Sniffy

THE VIRTUAL RAT
Lite Version 3.0 (with CD Rom)

Tom Alloway
University of Toronto at Mississauga

Greg Wilson
DID Software, Inc.

Jeff Graham
University of Toronto at Mississauga

WADSWORTH
CENGAGE Learning·

Australia • Brazil • Japan • Korea • Mexico • Singapore • Spain • United Kingdom • United States

WADSWORTH
CENGAGE Learning

Sniffy: The Virtual Rat Lite Version 3.0 (with CD Rom), Third edition
Tom Alloway, Greg Wilson and Jeff Graham

Senior Publisher: Linda Schreiber-Ganster

Acquisition Editor: Timothy Matray

Editorial Assistant: Lauren K. Moody

Media Editor: Lauren Keyes

Marketing Manager: Jessica Egbert

Marketing Communications Manager: Laura Localio

Content Project Management: PreMediaGlobal

Design Director: Rob Hugel

Senior Art Director: Pamela Galbreath

Print Buyer: Judy Inouye

Rights Acquisitions Specialist (Image): Don Schlotman

Rights Acquisitions Specialist (Text): Don Schlotman

Production Service: PreMediaGlobal

Cover Designer: Larry Didona

Cover Image: mouse: © Galushko Sergey / Shutterstock.com circuit board: © apdesign / Shutterstock.com

Compositor: PreMediaGlobal

Trademark Notice

For product information and technology assistance, contact us at
Cengage Learning Customer & Sales Support, 1-800-354-9706

For permission to use material from this text or product, submit all requests online at **www.cengage.com/permissions**
Further permissions questions can be emailed to
permissionrequest@cengage.com

Library of Congress Control Number: 2010943133

ISBN-13: 978-1-111-72617-1

ISBN-10: 1-111-72617-5

Wadsworth
20 Davis Drive
Belmont, CA 94002-3098
USA

Cengage Learning is a leading provider of customized learning solutions with office locations around the globe, including Singapore, the United Kingdom, Australia, Mexico, Brazil, and Japan. Locate your local office at **www.cengage.com/global**

Cengage Learning products are represented in Canada by Nelson Education, Ltd.

To learn more about Wadsworth, visit **www.cengage.com/Wadsworth**

Purchase any of our products at your local college store or at our preferred online store **www.cengagebrain.com**

Instructors: Please visit **login.cengage.com** and log in to access instructor-specific resources.

Printed in the United States of America
1 2 3 4 5 6 7 15 14 13 12 11

Dedication

To the laboratory rat

 # Contents

6   Schedules of Reinforcement **71**

7   Shaping Behaviors Other Than Bar Pressing **91**

Preface: Installing and Running Sniffy Lite

System Requirements

Windows

You need an IBM-compatible computer running Windows Vista Home Edition or later. The computer should have an Intel Core2 Duo processor (or equivalent), a minimum of 2 GB of random access memory (RAM), and a CD or DVD player.

Macintosh

You need an Apple Macintosh computer with an Intel Core2 Duo processor, running Mac OS 10.5 or later. The computer must have at least 2 GB of RAM and a DVD player.

Installation

The Sniffy Lite program is designed to be installed on the hard drive of the user's computer. It is not designed to be run from the CD or from a server. Attempting to run the program from the CD or from a server is likely to produce erratic and unpredictable results.

FAQ and Read Me Files

Before installing the program, read the FAQ and Read Me files that are included on your CD. It would also be a very good idea to check the Sniffy Web site to find out whether a revised FAQ file or an update to the Sniffy Lite program is available there. We will post a new FAQ file on the Web site whenever new information becomes available.

Windows

- Use your left mouse button to double-click the installer program called Install SniffyLiteSetup on your Sniffy Lite CD, and follow the instructions as you progress. The first screen that you will see is shown below.
- The installer will place:
  - □ The Sniffy Lite program inside the Program Files (x86) on your Local Disk (C Drive).
  - □ The Sample Files folder inside a folder titled Sniffy Data Files that is inside the My Documents folder (Documents Library) associated with your user name.
  - □ A shortcut to launch the program easily in your Start menu.
- You should save all your Sniffy files in your Sniffy Data Files folder so that they are all together in the same place where you can find them easily. When performing the exercises, there will be many occasions when you can save yourself time and effort if you have the file from a previous exercise available to use as the basis for a new exercise.

Macintosh

- To install the Sniffy Lite application, copy it from the CD into the Applications folder on you Macintosh's hard drive.
  - □ Double-click on your computer's hard drive icon, which should be located on your Macintosh desktop. If necessary, scroll around to make the Applications folder visible.
  - □ Point the cursor at the Sniffy Lite application icon on the CD, click and hold down your (left) mouse button, and drag the application icon into the Applications folder on your hard drive.

- We also strongly recommend that you create a folder called Sniffy Data Files on your hard drive and save all your Sniffy files in your Sniffy Data Files folder. When performing the exercises, there will be many occasions when you can save yourself time and effort if you have the file from a previous exercise available to use as the basis for a new exercise.
- To create your Sniffy Data Files inside your Documents folder:
  □ Double-click on the hard drive icon, which is probably located in the upper right-hand corner of your screen.
  □ Double-click on the Users folder.
  □ Double-click on your own User identity. Your Documents folder should now be visible.
  □ Double-click on the Documents folder to open it.
  □ With the cursor pointed at the interior of your Documents folder, hold down the Shift and Command keys and type the letter N to create a new folder inside your documents folder. Immediately name the new folder Sniffy Data Files.
  □ Once you have created your Sniffy Data Files folder, copy the Sample Files folder from the CD into your Sniffy Data Files folder. The Sample Files folder contains a number of Sniffy files that you may find useful when you are doing Sniffy exercises.

Contacts, Support, and Information

In the United States

In Canada

International

Information and Updates

For the latest information and updates, check out Sniffy on the Web at www.cengage.com/psychology/alloway

To contact the authors via e-mail:

Dr. Tom Alloway   tom_alloway@me.com
Dr. Jeff Graham   jgraham@utm.utoronto.ca
Greg Wilson   didsoft@rogers.com

Acknowledgments

We thank the many students, friends, and colleagues who have helped since the inception of this project in 1991. This is the fourth edition of the software, having implemented more realistic animations in 2000, and new animations and exercises in 2004. We appreciate the help and support of Professor Doug Chute of Drexel University, who was the first "outsider" to see Sniffy's potential and who helped bring it to fruition. We thank the CNN, Télée Quebec, and CBC news teams, who helped promote Sniffy as an ethical alternative to the use of live animals in teaching.

Many thanks go to our art director, Allan Sura, for designing and creating the Sniffy movements based on real video of a live rat (although he did have to push the creative envelope for some of the new tricks Sniffy can now perform!). We also acknowledge the artistic contributions of Professor Nick Woolridge in Sniffy's first releases. He worked on the initial animations of Sniffy and is responsible for the Sniffy icon.

We would especially like to thank the University of Toronto students who helped during the testing sessions in 2010: Bilal Butt, Debbie Fernandes, Arubah Nadeem, Roohie Parmar, Brinda Patel, Komal Siddiqui, and Rebecca Szeto.

We are grateful to the thousands of introductory psychology students at the University of Toronto at Mississauga who have used, over the past 19 years, early prototypes of the software in class.

We acknowledge the support of the principal and deans of the University of Toronto at Mississauga, who backed us in the early days before Sniffy attracted the interest of a publisher. We thank the many reviewers who helped refine and polish operational features and pedagogical issues.

Tom Alloway and Jeff Graham congratulate our coauthor, Greg Wilson, on his achievement in programming Sniffy Pro for the Macintosh and Windows operating systems. Greg tirelessly tackled the complex assignment of converting psychological principles into demonstrable artificial intelligence and did so while dealing with the complex technical problems of cross-platform development.

Finally, we thank all our Wadsworth Cengage editorial team, especially Alice S. Powers (St. John's University), Steven Mewaldt (Marshall University), Cynthia Barkley (California State University of East Bay), Alicia M. Doerflinger (Marietta College) and Robin Flanagan (Western Connecticut State University).

Quick Guide to Menus and Commands

This section provides a quick overview of the menu commands available in Sniffy Lite.

Preferences

The Preferences for the Sniffy Lite program appear in the File menu in Windows 7 and in the Sniffy Lite menu in Mac OS X.

Configuration Preferences

Environment Parameters

Animation Speed   Slow   ——○———   Fast

Sound Proofing   Quiet   —○————   Loud

☑ Move Sniffy to middle of cage when opening files

Use Defaults   Cancel   OK

- The Animation Speed slider controls how fast Sniffy moves when he is visible. Adjust it so that Sniffy's movements seem realistic.
- The Sound Proofing slider controls the loudness of the sounds that the program produces. Loudness is also affected by the general sound level that you have set for your computer.

- The check box next to "Move Sniffy to the middle of the cage when opening files" affects the program's behavioral randomization. **You should not remove the check mark unless you have a specific reason to do so.** One of the most important ways in which the Sniffy Lite program is realistic is by simulating the behavioral variability of real rats. When Sniffy learns something, his learning changes the probabilities of his various behaviors. With a check mark in the box, Sniffy's behavior is randomized each time a file is opened, a feature that means that you can use the same Sniffy file as the starting point for a number of experiments and still get a slightly different result each time an experiment is performed. If you remove the check mark, Sniffy's behavior will not be randomized each time a file is opened; and the degree to which the program simulates the behavioral variability of real rats will be reduced.

The File Menu

New	⌘N
Open...	⌘O
Close	⌘W
Save	⌘S
Save As...	⇧⌘S
Revert	⌘R
Export Data	
Page Setup...	⇧⌘P
Print...	⌘P

The File menu contains the standard operating system commands for saving and opening files: **New, Open, Save, Save As, Revert, Print**, and **Exit (Quit)**.

- **New** provides a new rat ready to be trained.
- **Open** brings up the dialogue box for opening files.
- **Save** saves the current file under its current name and in its current location on your hard drive. If the file has not been saved previously, a dialogue box appears so that you can give the file an appropriate name and choose an appropriate place to save it on your hard drive.
- **Save As** brings up a dialogue box that enables you to give the file a new name and choose another location on your hard drive to save the file.
- **Revert** restores the file to the state it was in the last time you saved it.
- **Export Data** produces a file containing the numeric data associated with the currently active window. These data files can be opened in most spreadsheet and statistical analysis programs. You can use this command with the Cumulative Record, Movement Ratio, Suppression Ratio, DS Response Strength, CS Response Strength, and Behavior Repertoire windows.
- **Print Window** prints the contents of the currently active window. You can use this command with any window except the Operant Chamber.

The Edit Menu

Undo	⌘Z
Cut	⌘X
Copy	⌘C
Copy Window Image	
Paste	⌘V
Clear	

- The **Undo, Copy, Cut, Paste**, and **Clear** commands are not implemented in Sniffy Lite.
- **Copy Window Image** copies a bitmap image of the contents of the currently active window to the clipboard. This command provides a convenient way to insert images from Sniffy Lite windows into a word processor document. To insert an image from a Sniffy Lite window into a word processor document:
  - ☐ Select the window whose image you want to copy by clicking on the window once with your (left) mouse button.
  - ☐ Execute the Copy Window Image command.
  - ☐ Go to the place in your word processor document where you want to insert the image.
  - ☐ Select the Paste (or Paste Special) command from the File menu of the word processor program to insert your Sniffy Lite image into the word processor document.

Experiment Menu

Design Classical Conditioning Experiment	
Design Operant Conditioning Experiment	
Remove Sniffy for Timeout	
Isolate Sniffy (Accelerated Time)	⌘I
Pause	⌘G
Mark Record	⇧⌘M

The commands in this menu determine the experimental conditions that are in effect during Sniffy Lite experiments and control certain other functions.

Design Classical Conditioning Experiment

Executing the Design Classical Conditioning Experiment command brings up a dialogue box that you use to set up classical conditioning experiments. Detailed instructions for using this dialogue box are given in Chapter 2.

Design Operant Conditioning Experiment

Selecting Design Operant Conditioning Experiment brings the dialogue box that you use to set up operant conditioning experiments.

Remove Sniffy for Time-Out

The Remove Sniffy for Time-Out command brings up the following dialogue box.

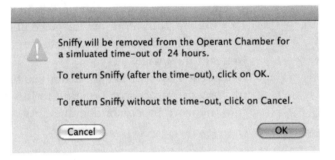

This command is used in experiments on **spontaneous recovery**. See Chapters 3 and 5 for detailed descriptions of experiments in which the command is employed. In the dialogue box:

- Click the OK command button to simulate giving Sniffy a 24-hour rest period in his home cage.
- Click the Cancel command button to dismiss the dialogue box without giving Sniffy a rest period.

Isolate Sniffy (Accelerated Time)

The Isolate Sniffy (Accelerated Time) command is available whenever Sniffy is visible. Executing the command replaces the view of Sniffy moving around in his operant chamber with the following graphic.

The graphic depicts the outside of a soundproof, air-conditioned chamber of the type that many psychologists who study operant conditioning use to isolate their easily distracted live animals from extraneous stimuli in the laboratory. Whenever this graphic is visible, your computer will run the current experiment much faster than when Sniffy is visible because the computer does not have to display Sniffy's movements.

Show Sniffy

The Show Sniffy command is available whenever Sniffy's isolation chamber is being displayed. Executing the command causes the Sniffy animation to reappear.

Pause and Resume

The Pause command is available whenever the program is running. Executing it causes program operation to halt until the Resume command is executed. The Pause command is helpful when something interrupts you while an experiment is running.

Mark (Record)

This command causes a small vertical mark to be placed just below the top of the Cumulative Record window to mark the fact that some event you want to record has occurred. For example, when training Sniffy to bar-press, you might want to mark the record to indicate the time when the Lab Assistant said that Sniffy's training was complete.

The Windows Menu

The commands in the Windows menu make specific Sniffy Lite windows visible. Selecting a window will reopen a window that has been closed or bring to the front any window that is currently obscured by another window. Note that the Cumulative Records, Mind Windows, and Lab Assistant windows are grouped in separate submenus.

✓ Operant Chamber	
Cumulative Records	▶
Suppresion Ratio	
Movement Ratio	
Mind Windows	▶
Lab Assistant	▶
Minimize Window	⌘M
Zoom	
Bring All to Front	

1

Introduction to Sniffy

Why We Created Sniffy

Sniffy Lite is an affordable and humane way to give students hands-on access to the main phenomena of classical and operant conditioning that courses on the psychology of learning typically discuss. Although psychologists believe that the phenomena that the Sniffy Lite program simulates play a prominent role in both human and animal behavior, courses that discuss these topics are usually taught in a lecture format that gives students no chance to obtain laboratory experience. There are two main reasons for this omission.

The first reason is cost. The most common apparatus that psychologists use to study classical and operant conditioning is the **operant chamber,** a special cage that contains a lever that a rat can be trained to press and devices for dispensing food and water and presenting other stimuli. A computer connected to the chamber automatically records the rat's responses and controls stimulus presentation. A basic setup consisting of an operant chamber, a computer to control it, and an appropriate interface between the two costs about $3500 in U.S. money. Few schools can afford to purchase this equipment in the quantity required to offer a laboratory component for a course in the psychology of learning. In addition, modern animal-care regulations specify rigorous standards for maintaining animals used for teaching and research. Typically, these regulations not only require that the animals be housed in clean cages and receive adequate food and water; they also specify that animal rooms must receive more fresh air and have better temperature and humidity control than rooms that people occupy. Facilities that comply with these standards are expensive to build and maintain. To cover these costs, animal facilities usually charge daily maintenance fees for each animal kept; these fees would add up to a large sum if each student enrolled in a learning course had his or her own rat to study.

A second reason why students in learning courses rarely have access to animals is that some people think that the use of live animals for teaching purposes, where the outcome of each experiment can be confidently predicted on the basis of previous findings, violates the ethical principles of humane animal treatment. Some people hold this view even when the animals used for teaching are never exposed to any discomfort. Opposition is much more widespread if the animals are subjected to noxious stimuli.

Nevertheless, studying animal learning without being able to see how experiments are set up and data are collected isolates students from an important and fascinating set of behavioral phenomena. The Sniffy Lite program is designed to end that isolation.

How We Created Sniffy, the Animated Creature

We created the animated Sniffy character that you see on your computer screen by videotaping a live laboratory rat as it moved around spontaneously in a glass cage with a blue background. The taping sessions occurred in a comfortable, reasonably quiet room, and we just let the rat perform whatever behaviors it happened to produce. From the several hours of videotape that we accumulated, we selected 40 short behavior sequences that show the rat walking around the cage, rearing up against the walls, grooming itself, and performing other typical rat behaviors. Finally, we removed the blue background from each frame of these video clips and adjusted the brightness and contrast in the resulting images to produce almost 600 animation frames that depict the rat in different postures and orientations. The Sniffy Lite program plays these frames in various sequences and positions to produce the virtual animal that you see.

Sniffy, the Program

The Sniffy Lite program lets you set up and perform a wide variety of classical and operant conditioning experiments and enables you to collect and display data in ways that simulate the ways in which psychologists do these things in their laboratories. In addition, because the program

both simulates and displays some of the psychological processes that psychologists believe animals (and people) employ, Sniffy Lite shows you some things about learning that you could not observe if you were working with a live animal.

In a real rat, learning is the result of biochemical interactions among billions of neurons in the brain. As a consequence of these physiological processes, animals acquire information about events in the outside world and about how their behavior affects those events. One aspect of learning involves acquiring information about sequences of events in the world. When one stimulus regularly precedes and thus predicts another, animals modify their behavior in certain ways; psychologists call this kind of learning **classical** (or **respondent**) **conditioning.** A second aspect of learning involves acquiring associations between behaviors (responses) and external events (stimuli); psychologists call this kind of learning **operant** (or **instrumental**) **conditioning.**

Although we believe that neurophysiological processes in the brain are ultimately responsible for the learned changes in behavior that we observe, psychologists generally discuss classical and operant conditioning in terms of the acquisition and modification of associations. To some extent, we describe learning in associative terms because we do not understand the physiological processes well enough to explain our findings fully in physiological terms. However, psychological and physiological processes also constitute different levels of explanation (Keller & Schoenfeld, 1950; Skinner, 1938). Thus, we do not need to understand the physiological processes in detail in order to explain learning in psychological terms.

To a degree, the relationship between neurophysiological processes and psychological explanations of learning is analogous to the relationship between the electrical activity in your computer's electronic circuitry and the simulated psychological processes that form the basis for Sniffy's behavior. Your computer contains the equivalent of several million transistors that are in some ways analogous to neurons in a rat's brain. The Sniffy Lite program uses the electronic circuitry of your computer to simulate the psychological mechanisms that many psychologists use to explain learning in real animals and people. One advantage of computer simulation is that we can program a computer not only to simulate certain psychological processes but also to display the simulated processes. This possibility has enabled us to develop a set of displays that we call **mind windows.** The mind windows show how Sniffy's behavior interacts with the events in the operant chamber to create, strengthen, and weaken the associations that produce

changes in Sniffy's behavior. Thus, the Sniffy Lite program not only allows you to set up experiments and record and display behavioral data in a fashion similar to the ways psychologists do these things, it also lets you observe how Sniffy's psychological processes operate. We think that being able to observe Sniffy's psychological processes will make it easier to understand how learning works.

Another difference between Sniffy and a real rat is that you can determine the nature of Sniffy's learning process in some situations. Because the psychological processes of real animals are unobservable, psychologists often perform experiments designed to enable them to infer which of two or more plausible psychological processes is actually involved in a particular learning situation. In a few cases, we have endowed Sniffy with the capacity to learn in two different ways. In these instances, you can determine which kind of psychological process Sniffy will employ in a particular experiment, observe the psychological process in operation, and see how your choice affects the results. In many cases, two different mechanisms will produce identical results. However, we will also show you some experiments in which the results will be different when Sniffy employs different learning processes. We hope that being able to see how the choice of a psychological process sometimes will, but often will not, affect the outcome of an experiment will help you understand how challenging a task it is for psychologists to design experiments that enable them to infer what psychological processes real organisms actually employ.

Sniffy Is a Learning Tool, Not a Research Tool

The Sniffy Lite program is the result of developments in computer technology that permit the simulation and display of complex processes on relatively inexpensive computers. However, the psychological processes and behavioral phenomena that the program simulates are characteristics of living organisms. Discovering those processes and phenomena required more than a century of research with animal and human subjects. Future advances in the scientific understanding of learning will also require research on living organisms. Sniffy Lite and other computer simulations are fascinating tools for demonstrating what we already know, but they cannot substitute for the real thing when it comes to acquiring new scientific insights.

Sniffy is not a real rat. In fact, Sniffy isn't even the most realistic simulation of a real rat that we could have produced. The Sniffy Lite

program uses a rat as a kind of metaphor to help you understand the psychology of learning. In designing Sniffy as a learning aid, we deliberately sacrificed realism whenever we thought that it got in the way of creating a useful learning tool for students. In addition to immediately obvious things like the mind windows and the capacity to choose which learning process Sniffy will employ in certain situations, here are some of the deliberately unrealistic things about Sniffy:

- You will be using food as a reinforcer (reward) to train Sniffy to press the bar or do other things in the operant chamber. Sniffy is always ready to work for food no matter how much he has recently eaten. In contrast, real rats satiate for food and stop working to obtain it when they have had enough. We could have simulated satiation but decided not to because satiation is mainly a motivational, not a learning, phenomenon. If you ever do research using food reinforcement with real animals, you will have to learn how psychologists control for this motivational factor when they design learning experiments. However, textbooks on the psychology of learning rarely discuss satiation, psychological explanations of learning phenomena make little reference to it, and we thought that simulating satiation would introduce a needless inconvenience for students of the psychology of learning.

- Real rats learn some things quite slowly. In an experiment in which an animal is taught to discriminate between the presence and absence of a stimulus by reinforcing bar presses when the stimulus is turned on and not reinforcing bar presses when the stimulus is turned off, a real rat requires several training sessions before the maximum difference in bar-pressing rate in the presence and absence of the stimulus is obtained (Keller & Schoenfeld, 1950). In contrast, Sniffy will learn the discrimination in less than an hour. Sniffy also adapts to changes in reinforcement schedules much faster than a real rat. Making Sniffy learn unrealistically fast in these situations gives you time to study more learning phenomena, and we thought that providing the opportunity to study additional phenomena was more important than realistically simulating the speed at which rats learn.

Applying What You Learn From Sniffy

The principles of learning that Sniffy illustrates have many real-world applications in such diverse areas as the therapeutic modification of human behavior and animal training for utility, fun, sport, or profit.

In addition to a thorough understanding of learning principles, effectively applying the principles of operant and classical conditioning to real-life situations nearly always involves large measures of creative ingenuity and finesse. To become a practitioner of therapeutic human behavior modification, you need to obtain a bachelor's degree in psychology, attend graduate school, study behavior modification under the direction of a professional, and fulfill the professional licensing requirements of the jurisdiction in which you plan to work. These educational and professional requirements have been established in an effort to ensure the effective and ethical application of the learning principles that Sniffy simulates.

Standards for would-be animal trainers are much less stringent. Anybody can purchase a puppy and attempt to train it. However, if you obtain a puppy and subsequently want to transform the unruly little beast that you actually possess into the obedient, well-behaved member of the household that you had envisioned, you would be well advised to enroll yourself and your puppy in classes at a reputable dog training school. As with human behavior modification, effective, ethical animal training involves combining a thorough understanding of scientific principles with ingenuity and finesse. The best animal trainers understand both the science and the art. Sniffy will help you learn the science, but you must acquire the art elsewhere. Failure to acquire the art before you try to apply the science can produce unexpected and sometimes even dangerous results.

2

Introduction to Classical Conditioning

A First Look at Sniffy Lite

The time has come to have a look at the Sniffy Lite program and to begin Sniffy's training.[1]

> - Locate the folder where you installed the Sniffy Lite program and sample files on your computer's hard disk.
> - Start the program.

Depending on whether you're running Sniffy Lite under Windows or the Mac OS X, when the program opens, your computer screen should resemble one of the following pictures. (If you are running older versions of Windows or the Mac OS, the appearance of the program and its associated windows will be slightly different.)

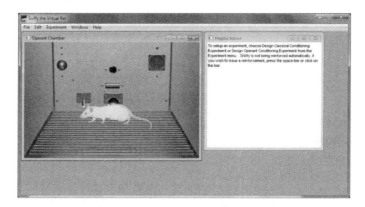

[1]In this manual, specific detailed instructions for performing particular exercises are presented with a gray background.

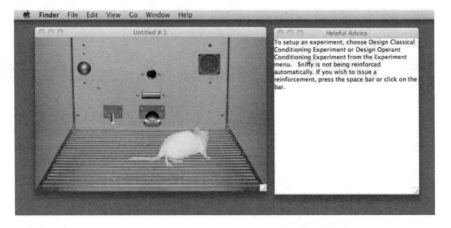

When you first start Sniffy Lite, two windows will be visible:

- The Operant Chamber window is the window where you see Sniffy moving about. The title bar at the top of the window contains the name of the Sniffy file that is currently being run. Because you have not yet saved a Sniffy file, the file is called Untitled in Mac OS X. In Windows, the window is called Operant Chamber.
- The Lab Assistant Helpful Advice window provides you with useful suggestions about what to do next or about the status of your current Sniffy experiment. In this instance, it is suggesting that to set up a classical conditioning experiment, you should select the Design Classical Conditioning Experiment from the Experiment menu, or to set up an operant conditioning experiment, you should select the Design Operant Conditioning Experiment command.

Throughout the rest of this manual, we will sometimes show illustrations of the way the program looks in Windows 7 and sometimes show how things look in Mac OS X. Because the program operates almost identically in both operating systems, always showing illustrations from both operating systems would be redundant.

Classical Conditioning Background

Classical conditioning is the form of learning that results when two stimuli reliably occur in a sequence so that the first stimulus predicts the occurrence of the second. Usually, the stimuli have differing degrees of biological importance to the organism, with the less important stimulus coming before the more important stimulus. Many of

the phenomena of classical conditioning were first described by the Russian physiologist Ivan Pavlov and his associates, who were the first to explore this form of learning systematically (Pavlov, 1927). Two other names for the same kind of learning are **Pavlovian conditioning** and **respondent conditioning.**

In classical conditioning, the stimulus that comes first in the temporal sequence is called the **conditioned stimulus (CS),** and the stimulus that comes second is called the **unconditioned stimulus (US).** The US initially possesses the capacity to elicit an obvious, easy-to-measure response called the **unconditioned response (UR).** The initial response to the CS is called the **orienting response (OR),** but the OR is often so inconspicuous that psychologists treat the CS as if it were a neutral stimulus that initially elicits no response at all. In other words, the OR to the CS is rarely measured.

The **classical conditioning acquisition procedure** consists of repeatedly presenting the CS shortly before the US. As a consequence of this repeated, sequential pairing of the two stimuli, the CS gradually acquires the capacity to elicit a new learned response, which is called the **conditioned response (CR).** Usually, but not always, the CR resembles the UR in the sense that the CR consists of certain components of the UR.

In their early experiments, Pavlov and his associates used food placed in the mouths of food-deprived dogs as the US. Food in a hungry dog's mouth elicits chewing, swallowing, and salivation as a UR. As CSs, Pavlov's group used various medium-intensity sounds, lights, and tactile stimuli, none of which had any initial tendency to elicit a response resembling the UR to food. When repeatedly paired with food presentation, all these CSs gradually acquired the capacity to elicit salivation. During the almost century since Pavlov first reported his findings, thousands of classical conditioning experiments have been performed, employing dozens of different species and a wide variety of different stimuli as US and CS.

The Conditioned Emotional Response (CER)

Sniffy Lite simulates a form of classical conditioning called the **conditioned emotional response (CER)** or **conditioned suppression.** Estes and Skinner (1941) were the first to provide the experimental paradigm for producing and measuring this form of classical conditioning. Sudden, intense sounds and electric shocks delivered to a rat's

feet are stimuli that intrinsically possess the capacity to interrupt a rat's ongoing train of behavior. The rat jumps when the loud sound or shock occurs and then freezes; that is, it remains motionless for a period of time. Thus, very loud noises and foot shock can be used as USs to produce freezing as a UR. In contrast, less intense sounds and moderately bright lights initially have little or no effect on a rat's ongoing behavior. For this reason, these stimuli can be used as CSs. The conditioning procedure consists of turning on the stimulus that is serving as the CS for a period of time before very briefly presenting the US. Usually, the CS and US terminate simultaneously. In different experiments, the period of time during each trial when the CS is presented by itself typically ranges between 30 and 120 seconds (Mazur, 1998; Domjan, 1998, 2003). The duration of the US is usually 1 second or less. As a consequence of pairing the CS with the US, the CS gradually acquires the capacity to interrupt the rat's chain of behavior and induce freezing.

Over the past 40 years or so, the CER has become the form of classical conditioning that North American psychologists most commonly study. There are probably two main reasons for this popularity. First, the CER provides an experimental preparation for studying the acquisition of a very important and interesting response—fear. Second, because the entire process of presenting stimuli and collecting data can be automated, the CER is a very convenient form of classical conditioning to study.

As originally described (Estes & Skinner, 1941) and in most present-day laboratories, studies involving the CER start by employing operant conditioning procedures to train a rat to bar-press for food or water reinforcement on a schedule of reinforcement that produces steady, rapid responding.[2] The rat's steady bar-pressing rate is then used as a baseline against which to measure the effects of presenting stimuli. However, because almost all textbooks on the psychology of learning discuss classical conditioning before operant conditioning, we thought that it was important to provide users of Sniffy Lite with a means of studying the CER before they learn about operant conditioning. Accordingly, Sniffy Lite enables you to measure fear-related freezing in two ways.

To measure freezing behavior in experiments where Sniffy has not been trained to press the bar, we employ a measurement called the **movement ratio.** This measure is the proportion of time during each presentation of the CS that Sniffy is manifesting freezing and other

---

[2]See Chapter 12.

fear-related behaviors. As the number of times the US has followed occurrences of the CS increases, the proportion of time during the CS when Sniffy will manifest fear behaviors increases. As implemented in Sniffy Pro, the movement ratio provides a robust behavioral measure of classical conditioning *whether or not* Sniffy has previously been trained to press the bar in the operant chamber.

The other way of measuring Sniffy's conditioned fear responses requires that Sniffy first be trained to press the bar in his operant chamber to obtain food reinforcement. This second measure, which is called the **suppression ratio,** is the response measure most commonly used by researchers who study the CER with live rats. The basic idea behind the suppression ratio is to compare the rate of bar pressing (the number of bar presses per minute) during the CS (Rate During CS) to the rate of bar pressing during the period of time immediately preceding presentation of the CS (Rate Pre CS). When the Pre-CS and During-CS time periods are of equal duration (as in Sniffy Pro), comparing the bar-pressing rates is equivalent to comparing the number of bar presses during the CS (Bar Presses During CS) to the number of bar presses during the period preceding the CS (Bar Presses Pre CS). If the CS elicits no fear response, the number of bar presses during these two time periods should be about the same. However, if the CS suppresses bar pressing, then Bar Presses During CS will be less than Bar Presses Pre CS. To get a quantitative measure of suppression of bar pressing in response to the CS, the suppression ratio is expressed as the ratio between the Bar Presses During CS and the sum of Bar Presses During CS plus Bar Presses Pre CS. Written as an equation, the suppression ratio is defined as follows:

$$\text{Suppression Ratio} = \frac{\text{Bar Presses During CS}}{\text{Bar Presses During CS} + \text{Bar Presses Pre CS}}$$

Let's think a bit about how this equation works. If presenting the CS does not affect the animal's bar pressing (if Bar Presses During CS = Bar Presses Pre CS), then the denominator of the fraction will be twice as large as the numerator; and the suppression ratio will be 0.5. However, if the CS suppresses bar pressing so that the rat presses less during the CS than during the Pre-CS period, the suppression ratio will be less than 0.5; if the rat doesn't press the bar at all during the CS, the suppression ratio will be 0. In a CER experiment in which the CS is being paired with an aversive US, Bar Presses During CS should rarely (and then only by chance) be greater than Bar Presses Pre CS, so that the suppression ratio should generally be less than or equal to 0.5. On the first training trial (before the animal has experienced the US), the

suppression ratio should be about 0.5. Then as conditioning proceeds, the value of the suppression ratio should decline until it eventually levels off at an average value less than 0.5. To compute the suppression ratio, the Sniffy Lite program compares Sniffy's response rate during the 30 seconds preceding each CS presentation with the response rate during the CS.

With real rats and with Sniffy, CER conditioning is rather rapid. Maximal (or nearly maximal) conditioning is reached after about 10 CS–US pairings. The US that the Sniffy Lite program simulates is electric foot shock delivered through the parallel metal bars that form the floor of Sniffy's operant chamber. Shock duration is always 1 sec. CS duration is always 30 sec. When the shock US is being paired with the CS, the shock US occurs during the last second of the CS.[3] Shocking Sniffy immediately interrupts Sniffy's behavior. He jumps and then freezes. When he begins to move around again, bouts of freezing are interspersed with bouts of grooming and exploratory behavior. After a few minutes, the effect of the shock wears off. If Sniffy has been trained to press the bar, bar pressing will resume. If Sniffy has not been trained to press the bar, he will resume moving around the cage and engaging in his other normal activities.

To animate Sniffy's UR to the shock US, we applied some tricks to sequences of animation frames derived from a videotape of a rat that had *not* been shocked or exposed to any other form of noxious stimulation. We think that the result looks plausible, but we do not know how realistic it is. Psychologists who study the CER virtually never give detailed descriptions of their animals' UR to the US. To create a realistic simulation of a rat's response to shock, we would have had to videotape a rat that was actually being shocked, but we did not do that.

The Sniffy Lite program uses a light as the CS. The light initially has no effect on Sniffy's behavior. However, when the light CS has been paired with the shock US, the light gradually acquires the capacity to suppress bar pressing and interrupt other aspects of Sniffy's behavior. When he is fully conditioned, Sniffy will begin showing bouts of freezing and other fear-related behaviors soon after the CS comes on. As was the case with the UR, although we think that Sniffy's CR looks plausible, we do not know how realistic it is because we did not videotape a rat that was actually being conditioned to manifest a CER.

[3]All stated times are in Sniffy program time. Program time is approximately equivalent to clock time when Sniffy's animation is set to run at a realistic-looking rate. However, program time and clock time will seldom be exactly equivalent.

The Design Classical Conditioning Experiment Dialogue Box

As noted earlier, one of the reasons for the CER's popularity among North American researchers is the fact that all aspects of CER experiments can be automated. A computer controls the presentation of stimuli, records the rat's behavior, and computes the movement ratio and/or suppression ratio. The Sniffy Lite program provides you with a simplified interface that enables you to set up and run basic classical conditioning experiments. Like a psychologist in a research lab, you will set up the experiment and then let your computer present the stimuli and record the data. When you choose the Design Classical Conditioning Experiment command from the Experiment menu, the following dialogue box appears[4]:

Classical Conditioning Experiment Design

Stage 1

Interval Between Trials

5 ⏺ Minutes

Present Each Trial Type

1 Times

New Stage

Delete Stage

First Stimulus

Light

Second Stimulus

◉ Shock UCS

○ None

Close   Run   ☑ Isolate Sniffy when experiment starts   ☑ Show Sniffy when experiment completes

- Classical conditioning experiments can contain one or more **stages.** A stage is a group of trials. All the trials in one stage are run before any of the trials in the next stage.
- In the Stage section of the dialogue box, the highlighted number that appears to the right of Stage indicates which stage of the experiment you are currently viewing. When you first open the dialogue box by selecting the Design Classical Conditioning Experiment command from the Experiment menu, the highlighted numeral to the right of Stage will always be 1, indicating that Stage 1 of the experiment is being displayed.

---

[4]The dialogue box is shown as it appears in Mac OS X 10.6. In earlier versions of the Mac OS X and in Windows, the appearance of the dialogue box is slightly different. All the program controls work in the same way in all versions of the Windows and Mac operating systems that the program supports. In this manual, we will sometimes illustrate dialogue boxes and data windows as they appear in Mac OS X and sometimes illustrate them as they appear in Windows 7.

- You can edit (create or change) any stage that has not already been run; and you can add more stages to an experiment in which one or more early stages have already been run. You can also view the settings for stages that have been run. However, you cannot change the settings for any stage that has already been run or for a stage that is in the process of being run. When you view the settings for a stage that has already been run or for the stage currently being run, all command buttons are dimmed; and you cannot enter any information into the text boxes.

- Clicking on the **New Stage** button creates a new stage, inserts it immediately after the stage that you were viewing when you clicked the button, and automatically moves you to the new stage. If necessary, other stages of the experiment are automatically renumbered. For example, if you have already created three stages and are currently working on Stage 2, clicking on New Stage will create a new Stage 3 and insert it between Stage 2 and the stage that was previously called Stage 3. The former Stage 3 automatically becomes Stage 4.

- The **Delete Stage** button deletes the current stage and, if necessary, automatically renumbers the other stages. Suppose that you have already defined four stages in an experiment and are currently working on Stage 3. Clicking the Delete Stage button will eliminate the old Stage 3 and cause the stage that had previously been called Stage 4 to be renumbered as Stage 3.

- You specify the average time interval between trials for the current stage by typing a number into the **Interval Between Trials** text box. Intervals between trials are measured in minutes. The number you type must be an integer (a whole number without a decimal point). The shortest allowable average interval is 2 minutes; the longest is 20 minutes. Remember that you are specifying the *average* interval between trials. The actual intervals vary from trial to trial so that Sniffy cannot learn to anticipate when the next CS is going to occur.

- The number you type into the box labeled **Number of Trials** determines the number of trials in the stage you are currently editing.

- To the right of the Stage section of the dialogue box are sections for defining the First Stimulus (CS) and Second Stimulus (the stimulus, if any, that comes after the CS).

- In Sniffy Lite, the first stimulus is always the light CS, and the duration of the light is always 30 seconds.

- There are two possible Second Stimulus settings: Shock US and None.

- Selecting the Shock US alternative causes the shock to follow every occurrence of the light during the stage that you are currently editing.

- Selecting the None second stimulus alternative causes the light CS to occur without the shock on each trial of the stage you are currently editing.
- Two buttons labeled Close and Run appear at the bottom of the dialogue box.
- Choosing **Close** closes the Classical Conditioning Experimental Design dialogue box and saves the experimental design settings.
- Choosing **Run** causes the program to run the classical conditioning experiment that you have set up.
- If you Quit (exit) the program or open another Sniffy file after executing the Run command, you will be asked whether you want to save the file. If you save it, the program will begin running the classical conditioning experiment exactly where it left off when you open the file the next time.

The Sensitivity & Fear Mind Window

Below is a picture of the Sensitivity & Fear mind window.

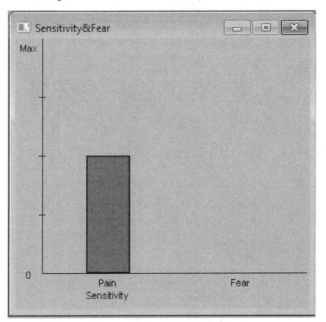

- Mind windows display internal parameters of the Sniffy Lite program that affect Sniffy's behavior. You should view them as representing Sniffy's psychological states. They are *not* measures of Sniffy's behavior. All mind windows have a blue background.

- The column labeled **Pain Sensitivity** depicts Sniffy's sensitivity to the shock US and predicts the strength of his UR the next time the US occurs.

- The column labeled **Fear** shows the current intensity of Sniffy's fear. Remember that this is not a measure of Sniffy's behavior; it is a measure of an internal program parameter that represents a psychological process. The more intense Sniffy's current fear, the more likely he is to display fear-related behaviors, such as freezing. If Sniffy has been trained to press the bar (or perform any other operantly conditioned response), he will be less likely to display that behavior when he is afraid. If Sniffy has not been trained to perform an operantly conditioned behavior, fear will reduce his exploratory behavior and other movements that are not related to fear.

The CS Response Strength Mind Window

The CS Response Strength mind window displays the strength of each possible light CS's capacity to elicit a CR as a function of trials. Below is the CS Response Strength mind window as it would be displayed at the end of a one-stage experiment in which the light CS was paired with the shock US 10 times.

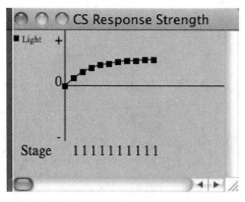

Please note the following features of this CS Response Strength mind window:

- The blue background color denotes that CS Response Strength window is a mind window, not a measure of Sniffy's behavior. The psychological state depicted is the strength of the light CS's capacity to elicit a CR at the end of each trial. CS response strength thus predicts how strongly Sniffy will respond to the CS the *next* time it is presented.

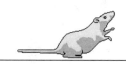

- The vertical axis of the graph indicates whether the CS response strength is excitatory (positive) or inhibitory (negative). The light CS has an excitatory, positive tendency to elicit a fear-related CR.
- Beneath the horizontal axis of the graph and to the right of the words "Stage" is a row of numbers that denote the stage of the experiment in which each trial occurred. In this example, the row of numbers consists of ten 1s because the experiment consisted of only one stage.

The Movement Ratio Window

Below is the Movement Ratio window for this same experiment.

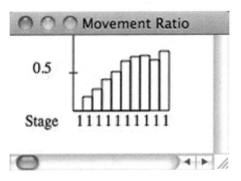

- The white background of this window indicates that it contains a measure of Sniffy's behavior. The movement ratio is the proportion of time during each CS presentation that Sniffy is frozen or manifesting other fear-related behaviors.
- At the bottom of the graph, the row of numbers that appears to the right of the word "Stage" denotes the single Stage 1 of this experiment.
- The movement ratio is 0 on the first trial. After Trial 1, the movement ratio increases rapidly and then varies at around 0.7 during the remainder of Stage 1. Thus, during Stage 1, the light–tone compound CS acquires the capacity to elicit a strong CER.

The Cumulative Record During Classical Conditioning

We believe that most users will conduct their classical conditioning experiments using a file in which Sniffy has not previously been trained to bar-press. However, for the benefit of those using files in which Sniffy has been trained to bar-press, we depict a cumulative record showing how the Sniffy Lite program records events during classical

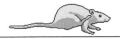

conditioning experiments. The cumulative record shown in this section depicts bar pressing during the last four trials of the experiment described above. In this case, prior to the classical conditioning experiment, Sniffy had been trained to press the bar in his operant chamber, and his bar-pressing behavior was being maintained on a VR-25 schedule of reinforcement, which means that he had to press the bar an average of 25 times to obtain a pellet of food.

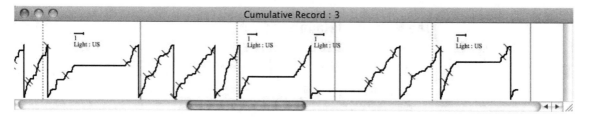

- The characteristics of the cumulative record as a measure of bar pressing and other operantly conditioned behaviors is described in detail in Chapter 5, Exercise 6.
- The cumulative record will not contain any useful information unless Sniffy has been trained to bar-press or perform another operant behavior. Users who are not using an operantly conditioned animal for their classical conditioning experiments should ignore this response measure.
- We strongly recommend that users who plan to use an operantly conditioned rat for studies of classical conditioning use an animal that is being maintained on a VR-25 schedule.
- Across the top of the record, the horizontal bars denote the times when the light CS was presented and its duration. The notation "1" indicates that the trials occurred during Stage 1 and notation Light: US indicates that the light CS was followed by the shock US. On the right-hand part of the record, the notation "2A" indicates that Trial Type A of Stage 2 was presented; and the words "Light" and "None" mean that the light CS was *not* followed by the shock US.

The Suppression Ratio Window

Similarly, for the benefit of users who are using an operantly conditioned animal for their classical conditioning experiments, here is the Suppression Ratio window for the same experiment. This response measure produces useful information only for animals that have previously been operantly conditioned.

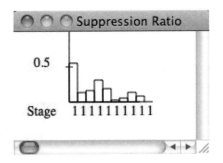

- The white background of this window indicates that it contains a measure of Sniffy's behavior.
- At the bottom of the graph, the row of numbers that appears to the right of the word "Stage" denotes the stages of the experiment that the recorded trials occurred during Stage 1 of the experiment.
- By chance, the suppression ratio is slightly above 0.5 on the first trial. After Trial 1, the suppression ratio decreases and then levels out at or just above 0 for the remainder of Stage 1. Thus, during Stage 1, the light–tone compound CS acquires the capacity to elicit almost complete suppression of bar pressing.

How to Get Reliable, Comparable Results

The movement ratio is a very robust measure of Sniffy's classically conditioned fear behavior, so robust that it provides a useful response measure whether or not Sniffy has been operantly conditioned to press the bar in the operant chamber or to perform any of the other operantly conditioned behaviors that Sniffy is capable of learning.

However, the suppression ratio depends on measured changes in Sniffy's bar-pressing performance. The Sniffy Lite program computes the suppression ratio by comparing the number of responses that Sniffy makes during the 30-second CS with the number of responses that he makes during the 30-second period just before the CS is presented. To make this measurement reliable, it is critically important that Sniffy be pressing the bar at a rapid, steady rate unless his response rate is being reduced because he is showing either a CR or a UR. If Sniffy is not pressing the bar at a steady rate, you will obtain erratic results because the value of the suppression ratio is affected by the number of bar presses that Sniffy makes during the 30 seconds prior to each CS presentation.

Variable ratio (VR) schedules produce rapid, steady bar-press performances that make ideal baselines against which to measure suppression ratios. Thus, we strongly recommend that you use a VR-trained Sniffy as the starting point for all your classical conditioning experiments that use the suppression ratio as a response measure.

The surest way to get predictable, comparable results both within and between experiments using the suppression ratio as a response measure is to use the same baseline Sniffy file as the starting point for all your classical conditioning experiments in which you want to use the suppression ratio as your response measure. The baseline that we used for calibrating the Sniffy Lite program is the VR-25 file located in the Sample Files folder. We recommend that you use it as your classical conditioning baseline in all experiments in which the suppression ratio is being used as your classical conditioning response measure. For experiments using the movement ratio as the response measure, we recommend that you start all your classical conditioning experiment with a new (that is, untrained) Sniffy file.

Your setting for the Average Interval Between Trials can also affect the reliability of both suppression ratio and movement ratio measurements. The default value for the average interval between trials is 5 minutes. When the low- or medium-intensity shock is being used as the US, that setting is almost always sufficient to ensure that Sniffy will have recovered from the effect of being shocked on the previous trial before the next trials occurs. However, recall that Sniffy's UR to the high-intensity shock sensitizes so that he requires longer to recover after he has experienced several high-intensity shocks. Thus, when the high-intensity shock is being used as the US, it is a good idea to use a longer average interval between trials. A setting of 10 minutes should almost always be sufficient.

Putting Everything Together to Understand Classical Conditioning

During a classical conditioning experiment, you can observe four things:

- **Occurrences of the CS and US.**
- **Changes in Sniffy's psychological states.** These changes are visible in the Sensitivity & Fear and in the CS Response Strength mind windows.

- **Sniffy's responses to the CS and US,** and especially how his response to the CS changes as a function of experience. You can observe Sniffy's responses to these stimuli by simply watching Sniffy's behavior during and after their presentation.
- **Response measures.** If Sniffy has been trained to bar-press or to perform any of several other automatically recordable operant behaviors, the Cumulative Record contains raw data about occurrences of the chosen operantly conditioned behavior throughout the experiment, shows when the different classical conditioning stimuli occur, and enables you to view the ways in which the stimuli affect Sniffy's operantly conditioned behavior. The Movement Ratio window shows the proportion of time during each conditioned stimulus that Sniffy is manifesting fear behaviors. The Suppression Ratio window contains the classical conditioning response measure that psychologists typically use in CER experiments.

Being able to see how stimulus events produce psychological changes that in turn produce behavior changes, which in turn are reflected in behavioral measurements, should enable you to develop a thorough understanding of the way in which psychologists believe classical conditioning works.

Exporting Your Results to Other Programs

During a classical conditioning experiment, the Sniffy Lite program enters data into the Movement Ratio, Suppression Ratio, and CS Response Strength windows. These graphs are saved as part of the Sniffy Lite file so that you can go back and examine your results after an experiment has been completed.

You can also export movement ratio, suppression ratio, and CS response strength results to a spreadsheet or statistical analysis program, where you can perform additional data analyses or produce more sophisticated graphs. To export the numeric data on which the CS Response Strength, Movement Ratio, and Suppression Ratio graphs are based:

- Click your (left) mouse button once while pointing the cursor at the Movement Ratio, Suppression Ratio, or CS Response Strength window.
- Choose the Export Data command from the File menu. Executing the Export Data command will bring up the standard dialogue box for creating and saving a new file.
- Choose an appropriate name and location on your hard drive for your data export file and click OK.

Printing All the Contents of a Data Window

You can print the contents of any response measure or mind window that the Sniffy Lite program produces.[5] To print the contents of a window:

- Select the window by placing the cursor over it and clicking your (left) mouse button once.
- Execute the Print Window command in the File menu.
- Make the necessary selections in the printing dialogue box that appears.

Copying and Pasting the Visible Portion of a Window

With the exception of the Operant Chamber and the Lab Assistant, the visible portion of all the windows that the Sniffy Lite program produces can be copied and then pasted into a word processing or graphics program that accepts pasted images. To copy and paste the visible portion of a Sniffy Window:

- Open your word processing or graphics program and determine where you want to paste the image that you are going to copy from Sniffy Pro. In a word processor, it's a good idea to go to the place in your document where you want to insert the image and create a blank line in the place you want to put it.
- Open the Sniffy Lite data file containing the window whose image you want to copy.
- If necessary, make the window that you want to copy visible by selecting it from the Windows menu.
- Make sure that the window that you want to copy is selected by clicking on it once.
- Execute the Copy Window Image command in the Sniffy Lite program's Edit menu.
- Move back to your word processor or graphics program.
- Execute the word processor's or the graphic program's Paste command, which will probably be under that program's Edit menu. (Some programs have a special Paste command for pasting images.)
- The graphic contents from the Sniffy Lite window will appear in the other program's document.

---

[5]The only window whose contents *cannot* be printed is the operant chamber, the window in which you see Sniffy moving around.

3

Phenomena of Classical Conditioning: Acquisition, Extinction, Spontaneous Recovery

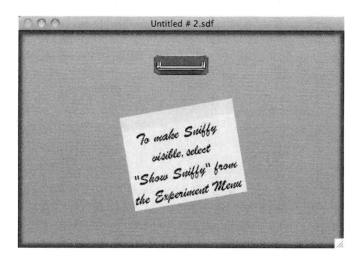

Warning: Don't let accelerated time get away from you. To save you time and enable you to perform a greater variety of experiments, the Sniffy Lite program contains a "time acceleration" feature. When Sniffy is visible, the program depicts all of Sniffy's movements. However, if you choose the Isolate Sniffy (Accelerated Time) command in the Experiment menu, the Operant Chamber window will display the image depicted above, and your computer will execute the experiment as fast as it can. The amount of time acceleration that contemporary computers produce is enormous. Sniffy experiments can last for a maximum of 20 hours of Sniffy program time. However, with Sniffy hidden, a reasonably fast computer may run through that amount of program time in less than 5 minutes of human clock time. The Sniffy Lite program has an important feature to help you avoid running time-accelerated classical-conditioning experiments longer than you intend. The Design

Classical Conditioning Experiment dialogue box contains two boxes labeled **Isolate Sniffy when Experiment Starts** and **Show Sniffy when Experiment Completes.** By default, both these boxes are checked with the results that: (a) Sniffy is hidden with time accelerated when an experiment starts and (b) Sniffy reappears and time acceleration ends when the experiment is completed. You should leave these default settings unchanged unless you have a specific reason to change them.

Background to the Exercises in This Chapter

Acquisition (learning) of a classically conditioned response is produced by repeatedly presenting the CS followed by the US. As a result of this acquisition procedure, the CS gradually acquires the capacity to elicit a new response (CR) that in most forms of classical conditioning resembles the UR. Once a classically conditioned response has been acquired, it can be eliminated by repeatedly presenting the CS alone—that is, without the US. Elimination of a CR by repeatedly presenting the CS without the US is called **extinction.** If the animal is removed from the experimental situation for a day or so after a CR has been extinguished and then returned to the experimental setting and given a second extinction session, it is likely that CR will occur again during the first few trials of the second extinction session. This reappearance of a previously extinguished CR is called **spontaneous recovery.** Early in the second extinction session, the CR is stronger than it was at the end of the first extinction session but weaker than it was at the end of acquisition.

Exercise 1: Basic Acquisition of a CR

Acquisition is produced by setting up a series of trials in which a CS regularly precedes occurrences of the US. The steps outlined below describe how to set up and run an experiment in which Sniffy receives 10 pairings of the medium-intensity tone CS with the medium-intensity shock US.

- If you plan to use the movement ratio as your measure of classical conditioning, simply start the Sniffy Lite program or, if the program is already running, choose the New command from the File menu.
- If you want to use the suppression ratio as a response measure, open a file in which Sniffy has been fully trained to bar-press on

a VR-25 schedule. We recommend that you copy the file named VR-25 that is located in the Sample Files folder, and use it as the baseline file for this and all your classical conditioning experiments that use the suppression ratio as a response measure.

- Use the Save As command in the File menu to save the file under an appropriate new name (for example, Ex1-ClassAcq) on your computer's hard drive.
- **Select an appropriate destination for the file on your computer's hard disk.** We recommend that you keep all your Sniffy Lite files together in a folder on your hard drive.
- Choose the Design Classical Conditioning Experiment command from the Experiment menu. In the Classical Conditioning Experimental Design dialogue box, make the following settings:
  - □ Be sure the numeral 5 appears in the text box located below Interval Between Trials, indicating that the average interval between trials will be 5 minutes.
  - □ In the text box located to the left of Times, type 10.
  - □ In the Second Stimulus panel of the dialogue box, make sure that the shock US is selected.
  - □ Make sure that a check mark appears in the boxes next to Isolate Sniffy when Experiment Starts and Show Sniffy when Experiment Completes.
  - □ Click the Run command button.
- Sniffy will then disappear, and your computer will run the experiment as quickly as it can.
- While the experiment is running, the Lab Assistant Helpful Advice window will give feedback about what is going on; and the CS Response Strength mind window will show changes in Sniffy's CS Response Strength.
- The response measure displayed by default will depend on whether you started setting up the experiment with a new, untrained Sniffy or with a file in which Sniffy had already been trained to bar-press. If you started the experiment with an untrained Sniffy, the program will display the Movement Ratio by default. If you started the experiment with a file in which Sniffy had already been trained to bar-press, the program will display the Suppression Ratio by default.
- When your computer has finished executing the experiment, Sniffy will reappear.
- After Sniffy reappears, save your results by selecting the Save command from the File menu.

During the next 50 min of program time, the program will automatically run the experiment. While the program is running, the Movement Ratio window will draw a bar graph that shows Sniffy's movement ratio as a function of trials. At the same time, the CS Response Strength mind window will produce a line graph depicting changes in the CS's capacity to elicit a CR.

At the end of the experiment, your Movement Ratio and CS Response Strength windows should resemble the following.[1]

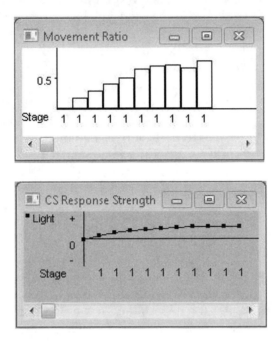

During acquisition, the movement ratio starts at 0 on the first trial, then rises and levels off at about 0.7. This increase in the movement ratio means that the tone CS is acquiring the capacity to induce freezing

[1]The CS Response Strength mind window should look exactly like that shown if you are running Windows 7. If you are running another version of Windows or the Mac OS, the contents of the mind window should look exactly like that shown, but the format of the window borders will depend on your computer's operating system. The contents of mind windows depict processes that are parts of Sniffy's learning algorithm, and these parameters are completely determined by the settings that you make in the Design Classical Conditioning Experiment dialogue box. However, the resemblance between the Movement Ratio window shown and the one you get will be less exact. The movement ratio is a measure of Sniffy's actual behavior. As Sniffy learns, the learning algorithm changes the *probability* that Sniffy will behave in certain ways but does not completely determine what Sniffy does. Because the learning algorithm only changes the probabilities with which behaviors occur, the details of the movement ratio result will be different each time the experiment is performed.

and other fear-related behaviors. As the movement ratio increases, the CS Response Strength mind window shows that the tone's capacity to elicit fear as a psychological process is increasing. Remember that the Movement Ratio window depicts a change in Sniffy's behavior, whereas the CS Response Strength mind window depicts the change in one of the Sniffy program's learning parameters that you might view as a "psychological state" that influences the behavioral change.

If you performed the experiment with a file in which Sniffy had previously been trained to bar-press, the Suppression Ratio window should resemble that shown below.

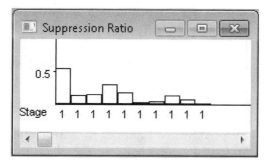

During acquisition, the suppression ratio starts out at approximately 0.5 on the first trial, then declines and levels off at an average value a little above 0. This decrease in the suppression ratio means that the tone CS is acquiring the capacity to suppress Sniffy's bar pressing. You could verify this fact by examining the cumulative record. During the last several trials, you would note that Sniffy stops pressing the bar very quickly after the tone comes on.

With a real rat, the animal's changing response to the CS would be the only thing that a psychologist could observe. Many psychologists explain this behavior change by postulating that it results from a change in an unobservable psychological process. With the conditioned emotional response, the acquired capacity of a CS to elicit freezing and to suppress bar pressing or other operantly conditioned behaviors is thought to be the result of an increasingly intense fear response. During CS presentations, Sniffy's Sensitivity & Fear mind window displays the strength of Sniffy's current fear; and the CS Response Strength mind window shows how strong the fear response will be when the CS is presented the next time. With Sniffy Lite, you can observe both the behavior change and the change in the Sniffy Lite program's classical conditioning algorithm—Sniffy's psychological state—that causes Sniffy's behavior to change. We have designed Sniffy's classical conditioning

algorithm to resemble theoretical processes that psychologists (for example, Guthrie, 1960; Hull, 1943, 1952; Rescorla & Wagner, 1972) have postulated in an effort to explain classical conditioning. However, nobody has ever seen anything analogous to CS Response Strength in a rat's brain; and many psychologists assert that it's impossible, even in principle, to observe the psychological (mental) processes of real animals. We believe that the Sniffy Lite program's mind windows will help you understand psychological explanations of classical conditioning, but it's important to remember that they do not provide any insights into the workings of the "animal mind."

An interesting thing to note is that the movement ratio and suppression ratio measures of Sniffy's response to the CS are not a perfect reflection of Sniffy's internal fear response. As the CS Response Strength and the Sensitivity & Fear mind windows show, Sniffy's fear response is at an almost constant high level during the last several acquisition trials. Yet the value of Sniffy's movement ratios and suppression ratios fluctuate somewhat from trial to trial. These behavioral measures vary because Sniffy's behavior is determined by a complex set of probabilities. Changes in Sniffy's learning algorithm (Sniffy's psychological state) change the *probabilities* with which fear-related behaviors occur, but Sniffy's behavior is always probabilistic and thus somewhat variable.

These variations in Sniffy's movement ratio and suppression ratio are somewhat analogous to the results that you obtain if you repeatedly perform an experiment in which you toss a coin 10 times. On any given coin toss, the probability that the coin will come up heads is equal to the probability that it will come up tails. For this reason, if you perform a great many 10-toss experiments, the average number of heads will be 5. However, the exact number of heads will vary from experiment to experiment. Sometimes you will get 5 heads, sometimes 7 heads, sometimes 4 heads. The operation of similar processes accounts for the variation that you see in Sniffy's response measures. The response measures vary because Sniffy's behavior is probabilistic. After every movement Sniffy makes, there are several things that he could do next. His experiences in the operant chamber change the probabilities of his behaviors, but the program is designed in a way that ensures that we can never know in advance exactly what Sniffy will do next. Even under very similar conditions, Sniffy doesn't always do the same thing. This variability in Sniffy's behavior is what accounts for the variability that we see in the classical conditioning response measures. The behavioral measures that psychologists obtain with real animals vary in a similar fashion and possibly do so for somewhat similar reasons.

Exercise 2: Extinction

These instructions assume that you have already run the acquisition experiment described in Exercise 1. To set up a series of 30 extinction trials, you should follow the steps listed. You need to give more extinction than acquisition trials because the CER extinguishes much more slowly than it is acquired.

- Start the Sniffy Lite program and open the file that we suggested you name Ex1-ClassAcq in which Sniffy acquired a CR to the medium-intensity tone CS.
- Use the Save As command to save the file under a new name (e.g., Ex2-ClassExt) in the Sniffy Files folder on your computer's hard drive. ***Saving the file under a new name preserves the original file in which Sniffy has been classically conditioned for future use.***
- Choose the Design Classical Conditioning Experiment command from the Experiment menu. The Classical Conditioning Experimental Design dialogue box opens to Stage 1. All the options for defining conditions are dimmed because Stage 1 has already been run.
- In the Design Classical Conditioning Experiment dialogue box, make the following settings to define Stage 2, which will contain your extinction trials:
  - ☐ Click on the command button labeled New Stage. The highlighted number 2 will appear to the right of the number 1 next to the word Stage. Because this is a new stage that has not yet been run, all the options for defining trial types are available.
  - ☐ In the Stage section, be sure that the numeral 5 appears in the text box below Interval Between Trials, and type 30 in the text box located to the left of Times. These settings indicate, respectively, that the average interval between trials will be 5 minutes and that the stage will contain 30 trials.
  - ☐ In the Second Stimulus panel, choose None.
  - ☐ Make sure that a check mark appears in the boxes next to Isolate Sniffy when Experiment Starts and Show Sniffy when Experiment Completes.
  - ☐ Click the Run command button.
- When the program has finished running the experiment, choose the Save command from the File menu to save your results.

During the next 150 minutes of program time, the program will automatically give Sniffy 30 extinction trials—that is, 30 trials during which the CS occurs without the US. As the program executes, the Sniffy Lite program will draw a graph showing Sniffy's movement ratio on each trial in the Movement Ratio window or the Suppression Ration window and the strength of the tone's capacity to elicit fear at the end of each trial in the CS Response Strength window. At the end of extinction, your Movement Ratio and CS Response Strength windows should resemble the following.

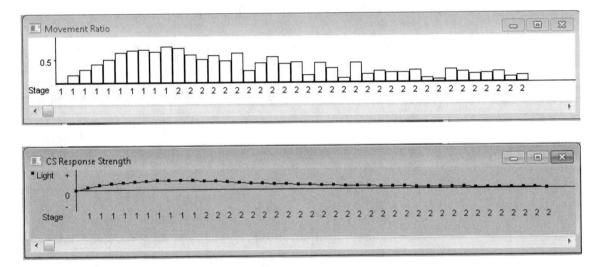

The Movement Ratio window shows that repeatedly presenting the CS without the US causes the CS gradually to stop eliciting freezing and other fear-related behaviors. The CS Response Strength mind window shows that this behavior change is the result of the CS's losing its capacity to elicit a fear response. Once again, note the variability in the movement ratio that reflects the probabilistic nature of Sniffy's behavior. If your experiment was performed on a file in which Sniffy had been trained to bar-press, the Suppression Ratio window should look something like that shown below.

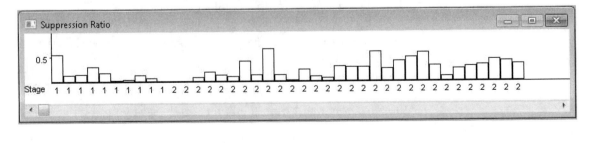

Exercise 3: Spontaneous Recovery

Here are the steps that you need to follow to observe spontaneous recovery.

- Open the file that we suggested you call Ex2-ClassExt from Exercise 2, in which Sniffy was first conditioned in Stage 1 and then extinguished in Stage 2.
- Use the Save As command to save the file under an appropriate new name (e.g., Ex3-ClassSponRec) in the Sniffy Files folder on your computer's hard drive.
- Under the Experiment menu, choose Remove Sniffy for Time Out. This operation simulates removing Sniffy from the operant chamber and leaving him in his home cage for 24 hours; a dialogue box will appear telling you that Sniffy has been removed from the chamber. To return Sniffy to the experiment on the next simulated day, click the OK button in the dialogue box.
- Choose Design Classical Conditioning Experiment from the Experiment menu and make the following settings in the Classical Conditioning Experimental Design dialogue box to give Sniffy a second 15-trial extinction session:
  - The dialogue box opens (as always) to Stage 1. All alternatives for defining trials and stimuli are dimmed because Stage 1 has already been run.
  - Click on the numeral 2 to the right of Stage to move to Stage 2. All alternatives for defining trials and stimuli are dimmed because Stage 2 has also already been run.
  - Click on the New Stage button to create the new Stage 3 after Stage 2. Note that a highlighted numeral 3 is now present in the number sequence after Stage.
  - Make sure that the Interval Between Trials is set at 5 minutes.
  - Set Times to 15.
  - In the Second Stimulus panel, choose None.
  - Carefully check your settings.
- Click Run
- When the experiment has finished running, save the file.

As Stage 3 executes, the movement ratio will be graphed as a function of trials in the Movement Ratio window or the Suppression Ratio window, and the strength of the tone's capacity to elicit a fear response

will be graphed in the CS Response Strength mind window. At the end of the experiment, these Movement Ratio and CS Response Strength windows should resemble those shown next.

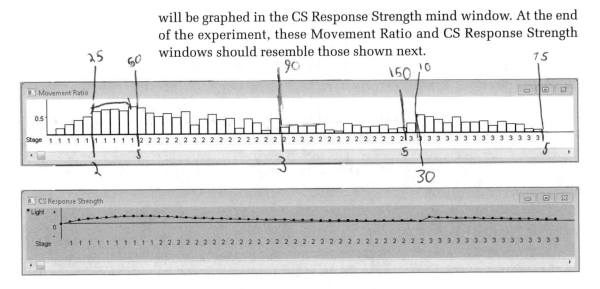

If you have been running your classical conditioning experiments with a Sniffy that was previously trained to bar-press, your Suppression Ratio window should resemble that shown below.

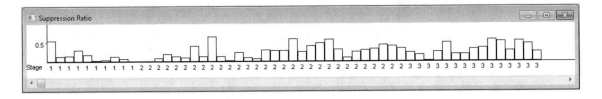

Some Questions

- Compare and contrast the movement ratio and the suppression ratio as response measures in classical conditioning.
- As the strength of Sniffy's fear response increases, the value of the movement ratio increases, but the value of the suppression ratio decreases. Why? How can two measures of the same thing move in opposite directions as the strength of the thing measured increases?
- Why do you think that most psychologists using live rats use the suppression ratio and not the movement ratio as their response measure?

4

Introduction to Operant Conditioning

Edward Thorndike

The research that led to the study of what today we call operant conditioning began more than a century ago with the work of Edward Thorndike. Impressed by William James's classic textbook, *Principles of Psychology* (James, 1890), Thorndike enrolled at Harvard University and took courses with James. At Harvard, Thorndike began the first experimental study of learning in animals. At the time, there was no formal psychological laboratory at Harvard and very little money to support Thorndike's work. His first laboratory was in his home.

Thorndike (1898) described his early animal learning experiments in a classic monograph. In these experiments, Thorndike studied the way cats learned to escape from an apparatus that he called a **puzzle box.** The cats were locked inside the box and had to manipulate a mechanical device to open the box and escape. Initially, the cats behaved in many different ways, most of which did not lead to escape. However, gradually, by trial and error, the cats found the behaviors that led to escape. Thorndike recorded how long it took each cat to escape on each trial and found that the average time gradually decreased from several minutes to a few seconds. As the escape speeds increased, the cats were learning to eliminate useless behaviors, while retaining the much smaller number of successful behaviors. The form of learning that Thorndike studied is often called **instrumental conditioning.** Thorndike summarized the mechanism that strengthens and selects successful behaviors by stating what he called the **Law of Effect:**

> Of several responses made to the same situation, those which are accompanied or closely followed by satisfaction to the animal will, other things being equal, be more firmly connected with the situation, so that, when it

recurs, they will be more likely to recur; those which are accompanied or closely followed by discomfort to the animal will, other things being equal, have their connections with that situation weakened, so that, when it recurs, they will be less likely to occur. The greater the satisfaction or discomfort, the greater the strengthening or weakening of the bond. (quoted in Kimble, 1961, p. 10)

Thorndike's experiments showed that the effect—the consequence—of a behavior determines whether the behavior will be strengthened or weakened. Hitting the right combination of levers in Thorndike's puzzle box had the positive effect of opening the door and letting the cat out of the box. As with most pioneers, Thorndike's models of instrumental conditioning and his statement of the law of effect have been subject to many changes. However, they remain an important cornerstone of our understanding of the learning process.

B. F. Skinner

B. F. Skinner formulated the methods and procedures that describe a variant of Thorndike's instrumental conditioning that Skinner called **operant conditioning.** In Thorndike's work with puzzle boxes, and subsequently in his studies of animals learning to run mazes, the learning tasks involved apparatus and procedures in which animals had the opportunity to make a correct response only at certain well-defined times called **trials.** Skinner developed a learning situation in which an animal is confined during training in a cage called an **operant chamber,** which contains a device on which responses can be made, as well as a mechanism, called the **magazine,** for the delivery of food. In an operant chamber, animals are trained in an experimental situation in which the opportunity to perform some response is continuously available. Like Thorndike, Skinner was interested in how the consequences of behaviors influence the frequency with which those behaviors are repeated. Skinner's work with operant conditioning is thus an extension of Thorndike's work with instrumental conditioning. Moreover, the same principles of learning seem to apply both when the animal has the opportunity to make a correct response only at certain times (as in Thorndike's puzzle boxes and mazes) and when the animal is able to respond at any time (as in Skinner's operant chamber).

Skinner (1938) made three fundamental assumptions about behavior:

- Animals are frequently active, a fact that means that organisms are continually **emitting** various behaviors.
- These emitted behaviors frequently have consequences that influence the frequency with which the behaviors are repeated in the future.
- The effects of the consequences are influenced by the animal's motivational state as well as by the physical and social environment. For example, the effect of presenting food as a consequence of performing some behavior depends upon whether the animal has been deprived of food.

Skinner studied animal learning, but he believed that it was possible to apply his findings to design more effective human institutions in which the planned, systematic application of reinforcement would make people happier and more productive (Skinner, 1953). Skinner not only called for the objective study of behavior, he also posited that behavior is often caused by events in the environment that can be discovered and manipulated to change behavior. In other words, he attempted to create a philosophical framework based on his findings; this effort generated a lot of excitement and controversy (Skinner, 1971).

Traditionally, people have believed that mental events cause many aspects of human behavior. In contrast, Skinner (1953, 1971) asserted that it is more useful to view feelings, thoughts, emotions, and most other mental events as covert behaviors. In Skinner's view, both overt behaviors and the mental events that accompany them occur because of current and past conditions of reinforcement, and both are subject to the same behavioral laws.

Although Skinner recognized that behavior is produced by the interaction of genetic and environmental factors, he and his followers have concerned themselves almost exclusively with environmental effects. The historical reasons for this emphasis on the environment are complex, but one important reason is that environmental factors are easier to manipulate than genetic factors, especially in human beings, in which genetic manipulations are usually considered to be unethical. Thus, for example, a child's genes and the environment in which the child grows up jointly determine how tall the child will grow to be. Although nothing can be done about a child's tallness genes once the embryo has been conceived, the diet that the child eats—an environmental factor—can significantly affect adult height.

Skinner (1938, 1953) stated that psychologists should be concerned with discovering the laws of behavior and emphasized the importance of relating environmental causes to behavioral effects. In addition, he believed it is often possible to discover behavioral laws without understanding what goes on inside the organism. Many psychologists have used the metaphor of a black box to characterize this aspect of Skinner's approach to psychology. The box, which represents the organism, is opaque. The inside is invisible, and we don't need to know what goes on inside the box. Understanding the rules that govern the box's behavior and controlling its actions do not require opening it. In fact, trying to understand what goes on inside the box may be confusing and misleading.

We can understand this "black box" view of the individual by considering the behavior of a television set. Few of us can produce or understand a circuit diagram that explains how a TV set works, but we can still operate one. We know that we must plug the set into an electric outlet. We know that when we manipulate the channel selector, the stations change. We know that a second control adjusts the volume, and other controls change the colors. The picture and sound are the behaviors that we want to predict and change, and we can predict and change these behaviors. If the set is not working properly, we also know that sometimes a sharp rap on the side of the case will improve the picture. None of this knowledge about how to change the behavior of a TV set requires understanding its internal workings. Skinner believed we can predict and change the behavior of organisms, including ourselves, in a similar way without needing to understand the internal workings of the body.

Skinner (1938) proposed that psychologists should seek to discover relationships between the environment and behavior without speculating about what goes on inside the organism. This "agnostic" approach to the workings of the organism was one of the most controversial aspects of Skinner's approach to psychology. A great many psychologists in Skinner's day (for example, Guthrie, 1960; Hull, 1943, 1952; Tolman, 1932) believed, and a majority of present-day psychologists still maintain, that understanding behavior requires understanding the psychological and/or physiological processes that go on inside the organism. A computer program manual is not the place to debate these profound issues in the philosophy of science. Suffice it to say that in designing a virtual animal that simulates the behavior of a real rat in an operant chamber, we had to endow Sniffy with certain psychological processes in order to reproduce the results that Skinner and others have obtained. Sniffy's psychological processes are modeled after

those discussed in many contemporary textbooks on the psychology of learning (for example, Domjan, 1998; Mazur, 1998; Tarpy, 1997). Nevertheless, there is no way of knowing how closely Sniffy's psychological processes resemble those of real rats. All we can say is that Sniffy's psychological processes, which we display in the various mind windows, illustrate the kinds of processes that many psychologists believe are characteristics of real rats.

Skinner (1935, 1938, 1953) distinguished between elicited and emitted behaviors. An elicited behavior is the specific result of presenting a particular stimulus. You studied how learning can affect elicited behaviors in the preceding experiments on classical conditioning. In contrast, emitted behaviors are responses that occur without any readily identifiable eliciting stimulus. For example, there is no stimulus that will reliably elicit grooming movements or barking from all normal dogs in the same way that placing food on a dog's tongue will elicit salivation.

Many of the behaviors that psychologists are interested in understanding are emitted, not elicited. Consider the behavior of students during class. They not only listen to the instructor and take notes, they also scratch, yawn, doodle, wiggle around in their seats, and exhibit a wealth of other behaviors. Almost all these behaviors are emitted in the sense that no single stimulus exists whose presentation will reliably elicit any of these behaviors from everyone.

The scientific question to which Skinner sought experimental answers was: What controls the frequency of emitted behaviors? To address this question, Skinner developed the operant chamber, a very simple environment in which he thought it would be possible to discover how the environment determines the frequency with which animals and people produce emitted behaviors.

The Operant Chamber

Sniffy's operant chamber resembles those found in laboratories where psychologists do research on operant conditioning. A look at Sniffy's operant chamber reveals three particularly important objects on the back wall: a lever, or so-called **bar,** that you will train Sniffy to press; a waterspout; and a food hopper. As in all operant conditioning situations, the bar is continuously available for Sniffy to press. The hopper is the device that you will use to provide a positive consequence, or **reinforcement,** when Sniffy does something that you want him to do more often.

You can program the operant chamber to deliver food pellets automatically when Sniffy presses the bar, or you can dispense pellets manually by hitting the space bar on your computer keyboard or clicking your computer's (left) mouse button while pointing at the bar. Other devices in Sniffy's operant chamber permit you to present other kinds of stimuli. These devices include a speaker through which sounds can be played, a light that can be turned on and off, and the parallel metal bars that form the floor through which electric shocks can be delivered.

In this restricted environment, a real rat performs a limited subset of species-typical behaviors. As with a real rat, you can expect to see Sniffy rearing up, grooming himself, and exploring the chamber. You can observe and record many of Sniffy's behaviors. However, the response that psychologists generally study in an operant chamber is bar pressing. In research laboratories, psychologists use computers to control the presentation of food and other stimuli and to record bar presses; the Sniffy Lite program simulates these functions.

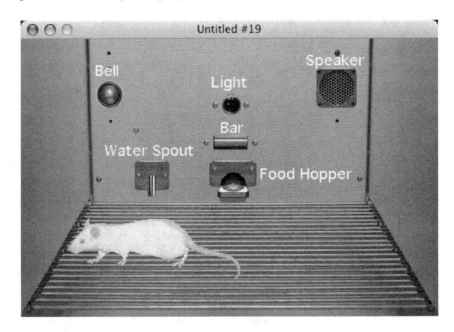

Reinforcement and Punishment

Skinner (1938) defined **reinforcement** as a procedure that makes a behavior pattern, or **response,** more likely to be repeated under similar circumstances in the future. In operant conditioning, the term *reinforcement* refers to the procedure of presenting or removing a stimulus (called a **reinforcer**) as a consequence of performing a response. A **positive reinforcer** is a stimulus whose presentation as a consequence of a behavior causes that behavior to occur more frequently under similar circumstances in the future. The term **positive reinforcement** refers to the procedure of presenting a positive reinforcer as a consequence of a behavior pattern. You will use food as a positive reinforcer to train Sniffy to press the bar or do certain other things in the operant chamber. A **negative reinforcer** is a stimulus whose removal or termination as a consequence of a behavior makes that behavior more likely to occur under similar circumstances in the future. The term **negative reinforcement** refers to the procedure of removing a negative reinforcer as a consequence of a behavior. Uncomfortable environmental conditions (temperature extremes, rain) are examples of negative reinforcers—stimuli whose termination can strengthen behaviors. As the saying goes, most people are smart enough to learn to come in out of the rain. Both positive and negative reinforcement have the effect of increasing the rate (the number of times per minute or hour) at which the reinforced response will occur under similar circumstances in the future.

Skinner (1953, 1971) decried the fact that much of our society is controlled by negative reinforcement. If we have a noisy neighbor in an apartment building, we may bang on the wall to make the noise stop. Termination of the annoyance is negative reinforcement for wall banging and will increase the probability of banging the wall again under similar circumstances in the future. Children do homework to avoid parental nagging, a woman visits her mother to escape her husband's abusive behavior, a worker shows up for work on time to avoid unemployment. Skinner believed that this heavy reliance on negative reinforcement is a sign of a poorly planned society. He wrote several books and articles describing how society might be better organized based on knowledge of operant principles and extensive use of positive reinforcement.

Operant conditioning also defines two procedures for punishing behavior. **Punishment** is the mirror image of reinforcement. Whereas reinforcement causes behaviors to be repeated more often, punishment causes behaviors to occur less often. A **positive punisher** is a stimulus whose presentation following the occurrence of a response makes that response occur less often in the future. **Positive punishment** is the name of the procedure involved in presenting a positive punisher as a behavioral consequence. If you hit your puppy with a rolled-up newspaper after it has a toilet accident in the house,

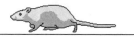

you are employing positive punishment. A **negative punisher** is a stimulus whose removal following a response causes that response to occur less often in the future. **Negative punishment** is the procedure involved in removing a negative punisher to make a behavior occur less often. If your daughter misbehaves while watching her favorite television program and you send her to her room (thereby terminating access to the television program), you are employing negative punishment.

Note that the terms *negative* and *positive* have the same meaning when applied to punishment that they have when applied to reinforcement. Both positive reinforcers and positive punishers have their effects, respectively, of strengthening or weakening behaviors when you *apply* or *turn on* the stimuli following a behavior pattern. Thus, the term *positive* in this context refers to the presentation or application of a stimulus. Both negative reinforcers and negative punishers have their respective effects when the stimuli are *removed* or *terminated.* Thus, the term *negative* in this context refers to the removal of a stimulus. But remember: Both positive and negative reinforcement cause behaviors to occur more often; and both positive and negative punishment cause behaviors to occur less often.

Another dimension that applies to both reinforcers and punishers concerns whether the reinforcing or punishing power of the stimulus is intrinsic or learned. Food is a good example of a stimulus whose reinforcing power is intrinsic; animals require no special training for food to acquire the capacity to act as a positive reinforcer. Similarly, presenting electric shock is an intrinsic positive punisher, and terminating shock is an intrinsic negative reinforcer. Stimuli whose effectiveness as reinforcers or punishers requires no special training are said to be **primary reinforcers** or **primary punishers.** Other stimuli that lack intrinsic reinforcing or punishing power can acquire the capacity to act as reinforcers or punishers if they are paired with primary reinforcers or punishers. Money is a good example of a stimulus whose reinforcing power has been acquired in this way. There is nothing intrinsically reinforcing about money; it's just pieces of paper and metal disks. However, people learn to treat money as a powerful positive reinforcer because of its pairing with primary reinforcers such as food and drink. Stimuli that acquire reinforcing or punishing power as a result of pairing with primary reinforcers or punishers are called **secondary,** or **conditioned, reinforcers** or **punishers.**

In operant conditioning, organisms learn that particular behaviors produce particular consequences in particular situations. In more technical terms, many psychologists believe that operant conditioning involves learning a three-part association among a situation, a response, and a reinforcing or punishing consequence (Domjan, 1998; Mazur, 1998; Schwartz & Reisberg, 1991; Tarpy, 1997). The effect of reinforcement is to select for the reinforced behavior at the expense of other, unreinforced behaviors. In other words, the effect of reinforcement is to make the reinforced behavior occur more often; a side effect of reinforcement is that many unreinforced behaviors occur less often because the animal or person comes to perform the reinforced behavior so frequently that less time is available to do other things. The effect of punishment is just the opposite of that of reinforcement. Punishment selects against the punished behavior, thereby making it occur less often and, as a side effect, making other, unpunished behaviors occur somewhat more often. An animal's **behavioral repertoire** is a list of all the behaviors that the animal would ever produce. The effect of operant conditioning is always to modify the relative frequencies with which different behaviors in the behavioral repertoire occur.

Skinner argued that punishment, in either of its forms, is undesirable for several reasons. Apart from ethical considerations, perhaps the most important of these reasons is that punishment is a less effective training tool than reinforcement because punishment conveys less information. When you punish an animal or a child for doing something, you are in effect teaching the subject not to perform one particular item in its behavioral repertoire in the situation where the punishment occurred, but punishment provides no information about which other behaviors are appropriate. Reinforcement is a more powerful training tool because reinforcement specifically teaches the organism what to do.

5 Basic Operant Phenomena: Magazine Training, Shaping, Extinction, Spontaneous Recovery, and Secondary Reinforcement

Operant Conditioning: Technique

Like a real rat, Sniffy will occasionally press the bar in the operant chamber even before you train him to do so. Thus, when you condition Sniffy to press the bar, you are not teaching him to do something that he was previously incapable of doing. Reinforcement simply increases the frequency with which bar pressing occurs. To train Sniffy to bar-press, you will administer a food pellet for each bar press. Thus, you will be using positive reinforcement to train Sniffy.

From what we've said so far, you might think that all you need to do to train Sniffy to bar-press is to set up the operant chamber so that the magazine releases a food pellet each time Sniffy presses the bar. In fact, if that's all you do, Sniffy will eventually learn to press the bar; but he will take rather a long time to do so. The reason for this slowness illustrates one of the most basic principles of operant conditioning: To be effective, reinforcement must occur *immediately* after the response. Delayed reinforcement is much less effective. The problem with food as a reinforcer in this situation is that even though a food pellet drops into the food hopper as soon as Sniffy presses the bar, the food can have no effect on Sniffy until he finds it; and Sniffy may not find the food immediately. When he does find it, the food will strengthen whatever behavior Sniffy was performing just before he found it, and that is more likely to be sniffing around the hopper than bar pressing.

Food is a very effective reinforcer that can be used to train animals to do many kinds of things, but it is often hard to deliver food fast enough to reinforce the response that the trainer wants to strengthen effectively. To overcome this difficulty, animal trainers often transform a stimulus whose timing they can precisely control into a secondary reinforcer by associating that stimulus with food. Then the trainer uses

the secondary reinforcer to increase the frequency of the response that the trainer wants the animal to learn. Fortunately, the magazine in an operant chamber produces a distinctive mechanical sound when it drops a food pellet into the hopper; and it is easy to transform this sound, which has no intrinsic power to act as a reinforcer, into a secondary reinforcer by pairing the sound with food delivery in a way that causes Sniffy to associate the sound with food presentation. The procedure that turns the magazine sound into a secondary reinforcer is called **magazine training.**

The Operant Associations Mind Window

The Operant Associations mind window displays the strength of three associations that Sniffy will learn when you train him to press the bar. To display the Operant Associations mind window, click on the Windows menu and then select Operant Associations from the Mind Windows submenu. In an untrained Sniffy, the Operant Associations mind window looks like this:

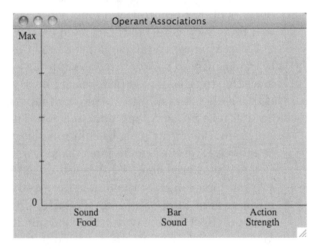

The Sound–Food Association

The **sound–food association** is the association between the sound of the food pellet–dispensing mechanism and the fact that a pellet of food is available in the hopper. You will teach Sniffy this association during the next exercise on magazine training. The **bar–sound association** is the association between the bar and the sound produced by the food-dispensing mechanism. When Sniffy is trained to press the bar, Sniffy learns that the bar is the device whose manipulation causes the sound that signals the presence of a food pellet in the hopper. **Action strength** is Sniffy's association between a particular behavior pattern and obtaining food. A strong sound–food association is a prerequisite for training Sniffy to perform any operant behavior. Action strength will also develop whenever Sniffy is trained to perform any operantly conditioned behavior.[1] However, the bar–sound association develops only when Sniffy is trained to bar-press. The bar–sound association doesn't develop when Sniffy is trained to do something other than bar pressing because none of the other behaviors that Sniffy can be operantly conditioned to perform involves doing anything with the bar.

The Cumulative Record

When you select Cumulative Record: 1 from the Windows menu of a new Sniffy file, the following window appears.

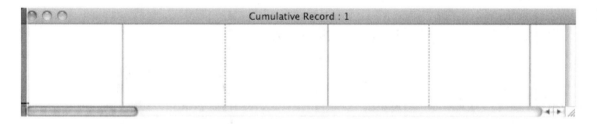

Cumulative records provide information about the timing of several different kinds of events that can occur during operant conditioning experiments. In the cumulative record, the spaces between the vertical solid and dotted lines represent 5-minute periods of program time. We will explain details about the features of the Sniffy program's cumulative record in future exercises. Here we simply note that the cumulative record is capable of providing information about times at which the following kinds of events occur:

- Times when you manually reinforce Sniffy by giving him a pellet of food.
- Times when Sniffy presses the bar or performs some other behavior that program has been set to record.

[1]In Chapter 7, we will show you how to train Sniffy to perform several other behaviors.

- Times when the program automatically reinforces Sniffy by presenting a food pellet after he has pressed the bar or performed some other behavior.

Exercise 4: Magazine Training

Magazine training is a technique that involves using what amounts to a classical conditioning procedure to turn an originally neutral stimulus into a *secondary reinforcer*.[2] The training process involves an interaction between you and Sniffy. What you will do depends on what Sniffy does, and Sniffy's future responses to the magazine sound will depend on what you do. The idea is to operate the magazine to present pellets of food in such a way that Sniffy learns to associate the sound of the magazine with the availability of a food pellet in the hopper. One of the associations that the Operant Associations mind window displays is the sound–food association. By keeping an eye on the Operant Associations mind window, you can watch Sniffy develop an association between the magazine sound and food.

Here are the steps that you need to follow to magazine-train Sniffy.

- Start with a new Sniffy file.
- Use the Save As command in the File menu to save the file under an appropriate name (e.g., Ex4-MagTrain) in the location on your hard drive where you keep your Sniffy files.
- Display the Operant Associations mind window by selecting it from the Mind Windows section of the Windows menu.
- Display the Cumulative Record by selecting Cumulative Record: 1 from the Windows menu.
- The message in the Lab Assistant window reads, "To set up an experiment, choose Design Classical Conditioning Experiment or Design Operant Conditioning Experiment from the Experiments menu. Sniffy is not being reinforced automatically. If you want to issue a reinforcement, press the space bar or click on the bar." The last sentence of the Lab Assistant message is the relevant instruction for this experiment.
- **Wait until Sniffy closely approaches the food hopper. Then deliver a food pellet, either by *pressing the space bar on your computer keyboard or by pointing the cursor at the bar and clicking your (left) mouse button.***

[2]The concept of secondary reinforcement was defined and discussed in Chapter 9.

- To save time at the start, you may want to give Sniffy several pellets in rapid succession before he wanders away from the hopper.
- Note that each time you give Sniffy a food pellet, a small vertical line appears on the Cumulative Record.
- After Sniffy has received several pellets, you can let him wander away a short distance before giving him the next pellet.
- Keep an eye on the Operant Associations mind window. When the height of the Sound–Food bar reaches about one-quarter of the way up the scale, the message in the Lab Assistant window will change to read, "Sniffy is developing an association between the sound of the hopper and the presentation of food. However, this association is not strong enough to properly train Sniffy. Continue to present food when Sniffy is near the hopper." Follow the Lab Assistant's advice. Continue to reinforce Sniffy when he is near the hopper.
- **Because you will want to be able to use this file as the basis for training Sniffy to perform several different behaviors, during magazine training do not consistently give Sniffy a food pellet after he performs any particular behavior or category of behavior.**
- When the height of the Sound–Food bar in the Operant Associations mind window reaches about three-quarters of the way up the scale, the Lab Assistant will display the message, "Sniffy appears to have developed an association between the sound of the hopper and the food. You can now use the sound as a reinforcer to shape Sniffy's behavior."
- Sniffy's magazine training is now complete.
- Save the file.

Exercise 5: Shaping Sniffy to Press the Bar

After magazine training, if the operant chamber is programmed to drop a pellet of food into the hopper every time Sniffy presses the bar, Sniffy's occasional spontaneous bar presses will be effectively reinforced, and Sniffy will learn to bar-press all by himself if you leave him alone. Moreover, he will do so much more quickly than would have been the case without magazine training. However, if you are

observant and have a good sense of timing, you can accelerate this learning process by using a technique called **shaping.**

Shaping is the technical name for a procedure used to train an animal to do something by reinforcing successive approximations of the desired **target behavior.** In this procedure, the trainer (teacher) leads the subject (learner) to progress by small steps. Reinforcement is delivered for progress and then withheld until more progress has been made.

To be a successful shaper, you have to be a careful and patient observer. Shaping works because behavior is variable. The idea is to pick a behavior that the animal spontaneously performs fairly often and that is similar in some way to the target behavior you want the animal to perform eventually. Reinforcing this first approximation of the behavior will cause Sniffy to perform that behavior more frequently. Because Sniffy's behavior is composed of movements that occur with different probabilities, you will notice a number of different variations. Eventually, Sniffy will perform a variant of the behavior that more closely resembles the target behavior. That variant then becomes your second approximation, and you require him to repeat that variant to obtain reinforcement. As the second approximation is performed more frequently, Sniffy will eventually emit another variant that resembles the target even more closely, and so on.

Shaping an animal takes patience, careful observation, and good timing. It is a skill that you learn with practice. Sniffy is easier to shape than a real rat, partly because he never becomes satiated for food and partly because his behavioral repertoire is smaller than a real rat's. Nevertheless, shaping Sniffy is challenging enough for you to get some idea of both the frustration and the eventual feeling of triumph that shaping an animal engenders.

In the Sniffy Lite program, bar pressing is part of a **response class** (a group of similar movements) in which Sniffy lifts his front paws off the floor while facing the back wall of the chamber. We programmed Sniffy that way because, in order to press the bar, Sniffy must first go to the bar and then rear up in front of it. Thus, as your first approximation to bar pressing, try reinforcing Sniffy for rearing up anytime he is facing the back wall of the chamber on which the bar and food hopper are mounted. Once rearing up facing the back wall has become more frequent, require him to rear up with his feet against the back wall. If your patience, observational skills, and timing are good, you should have Sniffy bar pressing frequently in less than 30 minutes. If you are very skillful, you can shape Sniffy in less than 15 minutes. However, if you are inattentive or have bad timing, you might have been better off letting Sniffy learn to bar-press on his own after magazine training.[3]

Shaping is such an attention-demanding task that you should not pay attention to anything but Sniffy's behavior while you are shaping. However, once Sniffy has pressed the bar four or five times in a minute, you can stop shaping him and watch the progressive effect of reinforcement as Sniffy presses the bar more and more often. At that point, you should start keeping an eye on the Operant Associations mind window to observe the development of the bar–sound association and action strength. The bar–sound association tells Sniffy that the bar is the device he uses to produce the sound that signals the delivery of a food pellet. The action strength is the degree to which Sniffy has learned that pressing is what he does with the bar to get the sound that signals the delivery of a food pellet.

Here is a detailed description of the steps that you should follow to shape Sniffy to press the bar.

- Open the file from Exercise 4 that we suggested you call Ex4-MagTrain.
- Select the Save As command from the File menu to give the file an appropriate new name (e.g., Ex5-ShapeBP) and save it in the Sniffy Files folder on your computer's hard drive. *Saving the file with a new name before you start shaping Sniffy preserves your original magazine-training file for future use.* You will need it for a number of subsequent exercises.
- If the Operant Associations mind window is not already visible, display it by selecting it from the Mind Windows section of the Windows menu.
- If Cumulative Record: 1 is not visible, make it visible by selecting it from the Cumulative Record section of the Windows menu.
- Select the Design Operant Conditioning Experiment command from the Experiment menu.
- In the dialogue box that appears, select Press Bar from the Shaping Behavior section of the drop-down menu under Recorded Behavior. After making the selection, click on the Apply button.
- Click the Close button to dismiss the dialogue box.

[3]Psychologists who study operant conditioning in live rats approach shaping in a variety of ways. Some people start the shaping process by reinforcing the rat whenever it approaches the bar. Others begin by reinforcing the rat whenever it turns toward the bar. Some of these alternative approaches also work well with Sniffy.

- Note that the terms CRF and Bar Press appear in the cumulative record. CRF stands for Continuous Reinforcement, which means that the program will automatically reinforce every bar press. The Bar Press notation indicates that the cumulative record is recording bar presses.
- As your first approximation to bar pressing, give Sniffy a pellet of food when he rears up facing the back wall anywhere in the operant chamber.
- Gradually require Sniffy to rear up closer and closer to the wall.
- Whenever Sniffy rears up directly in front of the bar, there is a chance that he may press it. If he does press the bar, he will hear the magazine sound, receive a food pellet, and the bar–sound association will start to develop. After several reinforced bar presses, a red column will appear above the words "Bar–Sound" and "Action Strength" in the Operant Associations mind window.
- When the column above Bar Sound in the Operant Associations mind window reaches about one-quarter of the maximum height, the message in the Lab Assistant window will change to read, "Sniffy is developing an association between the bar and the sound. Continue and Sniffy should be trained soon."
- Each time Sniffy presses the bar, watch closely what he does after eating the food pellet. He may press the bar again a second time either immediately or after rearing up near the bar a time or two. If he does press the bar again, you know you're making progress. Allow him to continue pressing the bar as long as he will do so. However, if he rears up more than twice without pressing the bar again, continue to reinforce rearing up.
- If you are patient, the time will come when Sniffy will press the bar 8 to 10 times in rapid succession. At that point, you can stop shaping, sit back, and watch the progressive effect of reinforcement as Sniffy continues to press the bar more and more frequently.
- Watch the rising levels of the Bar–Sound and Action Strength columns in the Operant Associations mind window. Sniffy's training is complete when the message displayed by the Lab Assistant changes to read, "Sniffy appears to be trained properly. You may experiment with different schedule effects."
- When Sniffy is fully trained, select the Save command from the File menu to preserve your trained Sniffy for future use.

After 30 to 45 minutes of attempting to shape Sniffy according to the instructions given above, Sniffy should be pressing the bar *at least* 20 times during each 5-minute interval delineated by the alternating solid and dotted vertical lines in the cumulative record. If your attempt at shaping fails to obtain that minimum result, something is wrong.

One possibility is that Sniffy has not been properly magazine trained. Look at the Operant Associations mind window. The Sound–Food column level should be *more than* three-quarters of the way up the scale. If it isn't, either go back and repeat Exercise 4 to create a properly magazine-trained Sniffy or use the file titled MagTrain from the Sample Files folder.

A second possibility is that you may not be reinforcing instances of rearing up toward the back wall as outlined above or not reinforcing these behaviors quickly enough.

For users who encounter difficulty with shaping, we have provided a section of the Reinforcement Action menu in the Design Operant Conditioning Experiment dialogue box called the **Shaping Tutor.** If you are having trouble reinforcing Sniffy's rearing behaviors:

- Choose the Design Operant Conditioning Experiment command from the Experiment menu.
- Under the Shaping Tutor subsection of the Recorded Behavior menu, choose Rear–Back and click on the Apply button.
- The Sniffy Lite program will now automatically reinforce all instances of rearing up facing the back wall, including all bar presses. Watch which actions the program automatically reinforces.
- When you believe that you are capable of effectively reinforcing these behaviors manually, reopen the Design Operant Conditioning Experiment dialogue box and choose Bar Press from the Shaping Behavior section of the Recorded Behavior menu, and Click the Apply button.
- If you are unable to reinforce Sniffy effectively by hand, watch what is going on as the program automatically reinforces rearing up facing the back wall. Once Sniffy presses the bar 8 to 10 times in a 1- or 2-minute period, reopen the Design Operant Conditioning Experiment dialogue box and choose Bar Press from the Target Behavior section of the Reinforcement Action menu. The program will complete Sniffy's training automatically.
- When Sniffy's training is complete, the Lab Assistant will display the statement "Sniffy appears to be trained properly. You may experiment with different schedule effects. I have set the bar to activate the food dispenser." Save the file.

Exercise 6: Cumulative Records: Visualizing Sniffy's Responding

In this exercise, you will learn how to interpret **cumulative records,** the means of recording and displaying a rat's bar-pressing behavior that B. F. Skinner (1930) invented. Although there is nothing specific for you to do with Sniffy in this exercise, we suggest you read the following paragraphs while seated in front of your computer with the program running so that you can look at Sniffy's cumulative record from time to time to check out the various features that we are going to describe.

- If the Sniffy Lite program is not running, start it.
- Use the Open command from the File menu to open the file that we suggested you name Ex23-ShapeBP in Exercise 5.
- If the latest cumulative record isn't visible, display it by selecting it from Cumulative Responses submenu of the Windows menu.
- Note that as time passes, the visible part of the cumulative record automatically scrolls to the right to follow Sniffy's current behavior. If you want to look at something that happened earlier, you can use the scroll bar at the bottom of the window to scroll back to the left. If you want to stop the cumulative record from moving, choose the Pause command from the Experiment menu.

How do we know whether a rat has learned anything as a result of training in the operant chamber? With Sniffy, you can observe the learning process directly in the Operant Associations mind window. However, when dealing with real animals whose psychological processes are invisible, psychologists treat learning as a process whose operation they must infer solely on the basis of changes in behavior.

Because bar pressing becomes more frequent as a result of training, Skinner chose to measure learning in the operant chamber as an increase in the frequency of bar pressing. To make the necessary measurements, he invented the **cumulative recorder.** Skinner's cumulative recorder was a mechanical device that pulled a long roll of paper at a constant speed under a pen that rested on the moving paper. At the start, the pen was positioned at the bottom of the record; if the rat did not press the bar, the pen would simply draw a long, straight horizontal line. However, every time the rat pressed the bar, the pen moved a notch upward toward the top of the paper. When the rat was pressing the bar, the resulting record was a sloping line that moved from the bottom edge toward the top of the record. The more rapidly the rat responded, the steeper the slope of the line. In other words, Skinner's cumulative recorder drew a record in which the steepness of the line was directly proportional to the rate of bar pressing.

The roll of paper that Skinner used in his cumulative recorder was not very wide. After recording a certain number of responses, the slanted line would reach the top edge of the paper. When that happened, the pen very quickly reset to the bottom edge of the paper, causing a vertical line to be drawn down the paper from top to bottom. This pattern of a slanted line working its way to the top of the paper, followed by a sharp straight line to the bottom of the page, gives a cumulative record the appearance of mountain peaks or waves.

These days, mechanical cumulative recorders of the sort that Skinner invented are obsolete. Scientists who study operant conditioning use computers to draw cumulative records of bar pressing in a fashion similar to the way the Sniffy Lite program produces them. We have described the workings of Skinner's original mechanical device because we think its operation is easier to understand than that of a computer program that simulates the device.

There are several important things to remember about the cumulative records that the Sniffy Lite program produces, and about cumulative records in general:

- The slope of the rising lines on the graph represents the speed with which Sniffy is responding. The steeper the slope, the more rapidly Sniffy was pressing when the record was made. If Sniffy is pressing the bar slowly, the slanted line will take a long time to reach the top of the paper, where it resets to the bottom. This will result in a record that looks like gentle, undulating waves. If Sniffy is pressing fast, the slanted line will reach the top faster, the pen will have to reset more often, and the resulting record will look like more and steeper waves.
- Reinforced responses are marked by short, oblique lines drawn through the record.
- If you let it run long enough, the Sniffy Lite program will produce a series of 10 Cumulative Record windows. The Cumulative Record windows, which are called Cumulative Record 1, Cumulative Record 2, and so on, are accessible under the Cumulative Records section of the Windows menu.
- Each Cumulative Record window depicts Sniffy's bar-pressing performance during two hours of Sniffy Lite program time. *Program time and clock time are not the same thing.* The relationship

between program time and clock time depends on both the speed of your computer and the animation speed setting. You can adjust the animation speed in the dialogue box that appears when you execute the Preferences command under the File menu in Windows or under the Sniffy Lite menu in Mac OS X. When the animation speed has been adjusted so that Sniffy is moving at a rate that looks realistic, program time and clock time should pass at approximately the same rates.

- The fact that there is a maximum of 10 Cumulative Record windows means that no Sniffy experiment can last more than about 20 hours in program time. After that program time limit has been reached, you can examine and save your results, but you cannot add any additional stages to that particular Sniffy Lite file.

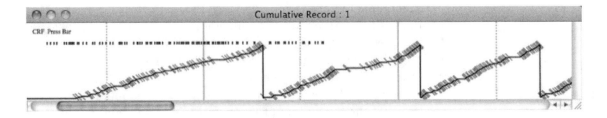

The cumulative record depicted above shows the acquisition of bar pressing as a consequence of shaping in a "typical" experiment. No two cumulative records are ever exactly alike, because Sniffy never behaves in exactly the same way in any two experiments. However, if you were a successful shaper, the part of your cumulative record from Exercise 5 that recorded Sniffy's acquisition of the bar-pressing response should resemble the one shown. Here are some characteristic things about the record shown above that you can expect to see in your own cumulative record:

- The notation CRF Bar Press denotes the time at which the program was set to reinforce bar presses. CRF stands for "continuous reinforcement," which means that the program reinforced every bar press.
- The short, vertical lines near the top of the record denote times at which the experimenter manually reinforced Sniffy.
- The flat, horizontal portions of the line show periods when Sniffy was not pressing the bar.
- Sniffy begins to press the bar somewhat slowly and intermittently at first, then more and more frequently and steadily.

- Note that the steepness of the cumulative record increases rather rapidly at first and then more slowly. A similar increase in the rate of bar pressing should be visible in your record. However, its relationship to pen resets is likely to be different.

Here are a couple of important features that are specific to the cumulative records that the Sniffy Lite program produces:

- The "height" of Sniffy's cumulative record is always 75 responses. There are always 75 responses between any two consecutive pen resets. When the pen resets the first time, Sniffy has made 75 responses. When it resets the second time, he has made 150 responses, and so on. Knowing this will come in handy later on when you need to figure out how many responses Sniffy has made.
- In addition to the dark vertical lines that the cumulative record produces when the pen resets from the top of the record to the bottom, there are thinner, alternating solid and dotted vertical lines spaced at regular intervals. These thinner vertical lines are 5-minute time markers. The time between one thin vertical line and the next (between a solid line and the next dotted line or a dotted line and the next solid line) is 5 minutes in Sniffy Lite program time; the time between two successive solid or two successive dotted vertical lines is 10 minutes in program time.

Exercise 7: Extinction

After training Sniffy to press the bar, you might wonder what would happen if you stopped reinforcing bar presses. This sounds like a simple question, but it reflects some of the complexity of life in a world where food sources come and go. Animals need to be flexible. They need to be able to learn what to do to obtain whatever food happens to be available at the moment, and they need to be able to stop doing things that no longer produce food. **Extinction** is the technical name for the behavior changes that occur when a previously reinforced behavior no longer produces reinforcement.

Here is what you need to do to set up and run an extinction experiment.

- If the Sniffy Lite program is not running, start it.
- Use the Open command under the File menu to open the file containing your trained Sniffy from Exercise 5.

- Use the Save As command to save the file under an appropriate new name (e.g., Ex7-Ext, for "extinction") in the place where you store Sniffy Files on your computer's hard drive. *This step is important because it preserves your original trained Sniffy file for future use.* You will need your trained Sniffy file for the next and other exercises.
- Choose the Design Operant Conditioning Experiment command from the Experiment menu. Executing this command opens the following dialogue box.

Reinforcement Schedule   Recorded Behavior

○ Fixed   [: | :]   Press Bar   [▲▼]
○ Variable   [1]   ○ Seconds
● Continuous   ⊙ Responses

○ Extinction   ☑ Mute Pellet Dispenser

(Apply)   (Cancel)

- When the dialogue box opens, the button labeled Continuous and the reinforcement action Press Bar are selected because you have been reinforcing all of Sniffy's bar-press responses. Reinforcing every response is a procedure called **continuous reinforcement.**
- To select extinction, point the cursor at the button labeled Extinction and click your (left) mouse button.
- Be sure there is a check mark in the box next to Mute Pellet Dispenser. (If the check mark isn't there, place the cursor over the box and click your (left) mouse button to put a check mark in the box.) Setting up extinction with Mute Pellet Dispenser selected means that Sniffy's bar presses will no longer produce food

pellets and that he will no longer hear the magazine sound as a consequence of bar pressing. In other words, both the primary reinforcer (food) and the secondary reinforcer (the magazine sound) are turned off. This is the standard extinction procedure.

- After checking to be sure that you have made the correct settings, click the Apply command button. The program will continue running, but Sniffy's bar presses will no longer be reinforced.
- If you want to speed up the experiment, select the Isolate Sniffy (Accelerated Time) command from the Experiment menu.

Immediately after you click OK, your cumulative record will look something like the one shown next. Note that the Sniffy Lite program marks the cumulative record to show the point at which extinction starts and informs you that the magazine sound is muted.

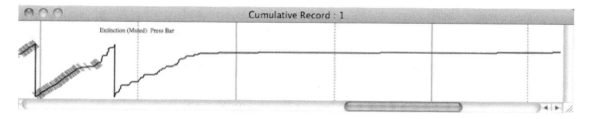

As a consequence of stopping reinforcement, Sniffy's rate of bar pressing will eventually decline until he presses the bar no more often than he did before he was trained. However, the very first effect of extinction is to *increase* Sniffy's bar-pressing rate. This brief increase in response rate is called an extinction burst, and it commonly occurs when an animal is switched from continuous reinforcement to extinction.

Your extinction criterion is a 5-minute period during which Sniffy presses the bar no more than twice. When that point is reached:

- Mark the cumulative record by executing the Mark Record command in Experiment menu.
- Save your extinction file by selecting the Save command from the File menu.

When the extinction criterion is reached, you should estimate the number of responses that Sniffy made between the onset of extinction

and the time when the criterion was reached. You should also estimate the time required to reach the extinction criterion.

When estimating the number of responses and the time elapsed during extinction, remember that:

- The thin alternating dotted and solid vertical lines on the cumulative record mark off 5-minute periods in program time.
- Sniffy always makes 75 responses between two successive pen resets.

Determining how many responses Sniffy has made during extinction and the time that extinction required will typically require you to estimate fractional parts of 75-response vertical pen excursions and fractional parts of 5-minute time intervals. You can elect either to make precise measurements or to do "eyeball" estimates.

If you want to make precise measurements, you should print your cumulative record and make the appropriate measurements with a ruler. To print your cumulative record:

- Select the Cumulative Record window by pointing the cursor at it and clicking your (left) mouse button once.
- Select the Print . . . command from the File menu.

To do an "eyeball" estimate, look at the cumulative record and estimate the appropriate horizontal (time) and vertical (response) movements as a proportion of 5-minute intervals and 75-response vertical pen excursions. For example, have another look at the cumulative record shown above that displays the point at which the change from continuous reinforcement to extinction occurred. The change occurred partway through a 5-minute interval between two vertical lines and partway up from the bottom of the cumulative record.

- With regard to time, the change occurred about 2/3 of the way through a 5-minute interval. Two-thirds of 5 is 3.35. So our estimate is that the change occurred about 3 minutes and 20 seconds into the 5-minute interval, so that about 1 minute and 40 seconds remained before the cumulative record reached the time marker.
- With regard to the number of responses that Sniffy made after the previous time marker and before the switch to extinction, it looks as though the cumulative record had moved about 3/4 of the way up from the bottom. We know that there are 75 responses between pen resets, which means that Sniffy had 18 to 20 responses to go before the pen reset again.

A couple of things about the standard extinction experiment are worthy of some discussion. One of them is the *extinction burst*—the increase in response rate that occurs immediately after Sniffy (or a real rat) is switched from continuous reinforcement to extinction. With real animals, the concept of *frustration* is sometimes evoked as an explanation. An animal that has become accustomed to continuous reinforcement expects to be reinforced for every response. When the expected reinforcement fails to occur, frustration, a hypothetical emotional state, results. This emotion supposedly energizes the animal to make a burst of responses.

With Sniffy, the explanation is much simpler. Sniffy does not manifest frustration. We know this because we did not model frustration in the Sniffy Lite program. When Sniffy is being maintained on continuous reinforcement, he hears the magazine sound after each bar press and comes down off the bar to eat the pellet of food whose availability the magazine sound signals. When Sniffy is switched to standard extinction, the magazine sound no longer occurs. Without the magazine sound to "call" him from the bar, Sniffy can do several things. He *may* come down off the bar and sniff the food hopper. He *may* also come down off the bar and do something else such as grooming himself or walking around in the operant chamber. However, in the first stages of extinction, the bar-pressing response is still very strong. Thus, the thing that Sniffy is most likely to do is to remain mounted at the bar and continue to press it again and again. Because Sniffy can press the bar faster if he doesn't come down to examine the food hopper after each bar press, his response rate goes up.

A second thing to note about the standard extinction procedure is that the Operant Associations mind window shows that extinction results in the elimination of the bar–sound association and action strength. However, the sound–food association remains intact. The bar–sound association and action strength dissipate because bar presses no longer produce the sound. The sound–food association remains intact because Sniffy never hears the sound without receiving a food pellet.

Exercise 8: Secondary Reinforcement

To get Sniffy to bar-press in the first place, you did two things. During magazine training, you turned the magazine sound into a secondary reinforcer by pairing it with food. Then during shaping, you strengthened an association between the bar and the sound. Finally, during standard extinction, you turned off both the sound and the food. In this exercise,

you will demonstrate the reinforcing power of the magazine sound by leaving it turned on during extinction. In other words, you will set up an extinction experiment in which Sniffy no longer receives any food when he presses the bar. However, bar presses will continue to produce the magazine sound (as if the magazine continued to operate when it contained no food pellets). Presenting the magazine sound as a consequence of bar pressing during extinction will have two effects. First, presenting the sound after each bar press during extinction will for a while continue to reinforce bar presses, with the result that the extinction process will be slowed down. Second, because the sound occurs but no food pellets are delivered, the sound–food association will eventually dissipate.

To set up the experiment, you should follow these steps.

- If the Sniffy Lite program is not running, start it.
- Use the Open command under the File menu to open the file containing the Sniffy that you trained to bar-press for continuous reinforcement in Exercise 5. (This is the file called Ex5-ShapeBP if you followed our file-naming suggestion.)
- Use the Save As command to save the file under an appropriate new name (e.g., Ex8-SecRef) in the Sniffy Files folder on your computer's hard drive. *This step is important because it preserves your original trained Sniffy file for future use.* You will need your trained Sniffy for future exercises.
- Choose the Design Operant Conditioning Experiment command from the Experiment menu.
- When the dialogue box opens, point the cursor at the button labeled Extinction and click your (left) mouse button to select that option.
- Then point the cursor at the box next to Mute Pellet Dispenser and click it to uncheck this option. Setting up extinction with Mute Pellet Dispenser turned off means that Sniffy's bar presses will no longer produce food pellets, but he will continue to hear the magazine sound as a consequence of bar pressing. The primary reinforcer (food) is turned off, but the secondary reinforcer (the magazine sound) remains on.
- After checking to be sure that you have made the correct settings, click the Apply command button.
- Click the Close button to dismiss the dialogue box.
- If you want to speed up the experiment, select the Isolate Sniffy (Accelerate Time) command from the Experiment menu.

Immediately after clicking OK, your cumulative record will look something like that shown next. Note that the Sniffy Lite program marks the cumulative record to show the point at which extinction starts and informs you that the magazine is not muted.

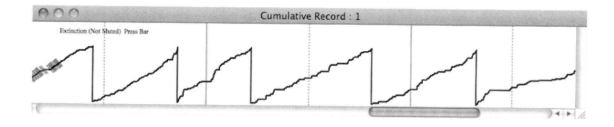

Because Sniffy hears the magazine sound after each bar press, we no longer see the *extinction burst*, the initial increase in the rate of bar pressing that we saw during standard extinction without the magazine sound. Each time he hears the magazine sound, Sniffy comes down off the bar and sniffs at the food hopper.

Your extinction criterion is a 5-minute period during which Sniffy presses the bar no more than twice. When that point is reached:

- Save your Secondary Reinforcement file.

When the extinction criterion is reached, you should estimate the number of responses that Sniffy made between the onset of extinction and the time when the criterion was reached and the time required to reach the extinction criterion.

Compare Sniffy's extinction with the magazine sound turned on with the extinction that you observed in the previous exercise. This comparison will reveal that Sniffy makes many more responses and that the extinction process takes much longer when the magazine sound remains on than when it is muted. This difference is caused by the initial secondary reinforcing power of the magazine sound when it occurs during extinction.

Finally, note that after extinction with the magazine sound turned on, the sound–food association extinguished, but the bar–sound association did not. The sound–food association dissipates because the sound occurs but no food pellet is presented. The bar–sound association remains intact because Sniffy continues to hear the sound after each bar press.

Exercise 9: Spontaneous Recovery

A single extinction session is not enough to reduce permanently the frequency of an operant response to its pre-training frequency. If an animal that has apparently been fully extinguished is removed from the operant chamber, allowed to rest in its home cage for 24 hours, and then returned to the operant chamber for a second extinction session, its response rate at the start of the second session will be greater than it was at the end of the first extinction session. This rest-produced reappearance of an extinguished operant response is called **spontaneous recovery.**

To simulate the phenomenon with Sniffy:

- Open a file in which Sniffy has been trained to press the bar and then extinguished. Either your Ex7-Ext or your Ex8-SecRef file will work for this purpose.
- Use the Save As command to save the file under a new appropriate name (e.g., Ex9-SponRec) in the Sniffy Files folder on your computer's hard drive.
- Choose Remove Sniffy for Time-Out from the Experiment menu. To simulate taking a rest, Sniffy will disappear.
- Click the OK button in the dialogue box.
- If you want to speed up the experiment, select the Isolate Sniffy (Accelerate Time) command from the Experiment menu.

When Sniffy reappears, his bar-pressing rate will be higher than it was at the end of extinction, but lower than it was before extinction. Immediately after the timeout, your cumulative record should resemble that shown below.

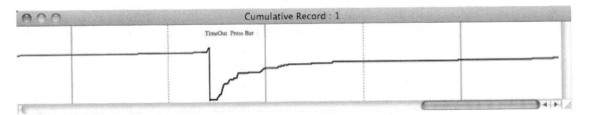

Check the Operant Associations mind window shortly after starting your spontaneous recovery experiment. You'll recall that standard extinction (with the magazine sound muted) produces extinction of the bar–sound association and action strength, whereas extinction with the magazine sound not muted causes extinction of the sound–food association. At the beginning of the spontaneous recovery experiment, the extinguished items are partly restored. This partial reappearance of the extinguished items is the "psychological" reason why Sniffy presses the bar more often at the beginning of the second extinction session than he did at the end of the first extinction session.

Let the Sniffy Lite program run until Sniffy meets the extinction criterion again. Compare the number of responses made and the time required to reach the extinction criterion during this second extinction session with the number of responses and time required during the first extinction session. This comparison will reveal that the second time around Sniffy makes fewer responses and takes less time to reach the criterion.

Sniffy's Behavioral Repertoire

An animal's behavior repertoire in a given situation is a list of the different behaviors that the animal ever performs in that situation. The Sniffy program is capable of recording how frequently Sniffy performs each of 22 different categories of behavior. Some of these behaviors are things that Sniffy does only after special training to do "tricks" that are described in Chapter 7.

To see a list of the behavior categories,

- Select the Behavior Repertoire item under Lab Assistant in the Windows menu.
- Then click on the arrow in the upper right-hand corner of the Behavior Repertoire window.
- Clicking the arrow causes a window entitled Behaviors to Track to appear that contains a numbered list of all Sniffy's behavior categories. The numbers in the list correspond to the numbers that appear along the horizontal axis of the graph in the Behavior Repertoire window. As a default, a check mark appears in the box next to each of the behavior categories listed in the Behaviors to Track window.
- If you do not want the program to record some of Sniffy's behaviors, remove the check marks next to the items that you do not want to record.
- When you have decided which behaviors you want the program to record, click the Apply button in the Behaviors to Track window.
- You can close the window by clicking the Close button.

When you record the behaviors that Sniffy is producing, the graph that Behavior Repertoire window displays shows the relative frequencies of the different behavior categories (that is, the proportion of Sniffy's behaviors that each category represents). Clicking on the

Record button in the lower right-hand corner of the Behavior Repertoire window causes the program to start recording Sniffy's behaviors and causes the label on the button to change to Stop. Clicking on the Stop button then stops the recording.

The graph in the Behavior Repertoire window provides a visual summary of what Sniffy is doing. However, to examine the frequencies of Sniffy's behavior in detail, you need to export the numeric data that the program records.

- To export the behavior–frequency data that you have recorded, make sure that the Behavior Repertoire window is selected by clicking on it.
- Then select the Export Data command under the File menu.
- Give your data-export file a name, and save it.

The exported data file can be opened using Microsoft Excel, Apple Numbers, and most other spreadsheet and data-analysis programs. When you open an exported behavior repertoire file with a spreadsheet program, the data will look somewhat like that shown below.

	A	B	C	D	E
1	Behaviour Rates				
2	Start Time: 28	End Time: 349	Duration: 3467 Seconds		
3	Behaviour	Times	Rate	Relative Frequency	
4	1) Rear - Front	84	0.024228	0.020953	
5	2) Rear - Back	141	0.040669	0.035171	
6	3) Rear - Side	26	0.007499	0.006485	
7	4) Groom Face	329	0.094895	0.082065	
8	5) Groom Genitals	190	0.054802	0.047393	
9	6) Tuck Head	0	0	0	
10	7) Turn	1982	0.571676	0.494388	
11	8) Walk	563	0.162388	0.140434	
12	9) Sniff Hopper	6	0.001731	0.001497	
13	10) Eat Pellet	0	0	0	
14	11) Drink	11	0.003173	0.002744	
15	12) Sniff	672	0.193828	0.167623	
16	13) Fear Freeze	0	0	0	
17	14) Pain	0	0	0	
18	15) Press Bar	3	0.000865	0.000748	
19	16) Beg	0	0	0	
20	17) Roll	0	0	0	
21	18) Wipe Face	0	0	0	
22	19) Pause at Bar	0	0	0	
23	20) Dismount Bar	2	0.000577	0.000499	
24	21) Pause Raised	0	0	0	
25	22) Dismount Beg	0	0	0	
26					
27					

Naive Repertoire

- Row 2 in the spreadsheet contains the Start Time and End Time of the recording measured in game time seconds since the beginning of the experiment and the Duration of the recording in game time seconds.
- Below these times are the behavior recordings.
- Column A in the spreadsheet contains a numbered list of Sniffy's behaviors. These names and numbers correspond to the names and numbers in the Behavior Repertoire and the Behaviors to Track windows.
- Column B contains the total number of *Times* that Sniffy performed each behavior while the recording was being made.
- Column C contains the *Rate* at which Sniffy was performing each behavior (the total number of times a behavior was performed divided by the number of seconds in the recording).
- Column D contains the *Relative Frequency* of each behavior (the number of times a behavior was performed divided by the total number of behaviors recorded during the session). Note that the relative frequency measure can theoretically range from zero (Sniffy never performs the behavior in question) to 1 (Sniffy never did anything else).

Exercise 10: Effects of Acquisition and Extinction on the Relative Frequencies of Sniffy's Behaviors

The items in the behavioral repertoire of an untrained, naive Sniffy can be categorized into eight major components[4]:

- **Paw lifting:** Sniffy lifts his front paws off the floor anywhere in the operant chamber. This broad category includes items 1, 2, and 3 in the Behavior Repertoire graph, which are called Rear – Front, Rear – Back, and Rear – Side in the behavior list.
- **Face grooming:** Sniffy touches his face with one of his front paws. This behavior is item 4 in the Behavior Repertoire graph and is called Groom Face in the behavior list.
- **Genital grooming:** Sniffy lowers his head down between his back legs as if he were licking his genitals. This behavior is item 5 in the Behavior Repertoire graph, which is called Groom Genitals in the behavior list.
- **Sniffing:** Sniffy stands with all four paws on the floor and twitches his whiskers. You can see his whiskers twitch when he is facing either toward you or toward the left or right wall of the operant chamber. When he is facing the back wall, you can't see his whiskers, but you

---

[4]These behavior categories of a naïve Sniffy do not include things that he can be trained to do but never does without special training.

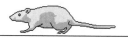

can see him wiggling a bit. This is item 12 in the Behavior Repertoire graph and is called Sniff in the behavior list.

- **Locomotion:** Sniffy walks around or turns his body. This broad category includes items 7 and 8 in the Behavior Repertoire graph, which are called Turn and Walk in the behavior list.
- **Bar pressing:** Sniffy presses the bar and sometimes comes down afterward. This broad category comprises items 15 and 20 in the Behavior Repertoire graph, which are called Press Bar and Dismount Bar in the behavior list. Sniffy presses the bar occasionally even when he has never been trained to do so.[5]
- **Hopper sniffing and eating:** Sniffy sticks his snout into the food hopper. If a food pellet is there, he eats it. This broad category includes items 9 and 10 in the Behavior Repertoire graph. These items are called, respectively, Sniff Hopper and Eat Pellet in the behavior list.
- **Drinking:** Sniffy places his mouth near the side or end of the drinking spout and makes licking movements. This is item 11 in the Behavior Repertoire graph, which is called Drink in the behavior list.

In this exercise, you will compare the relative frequencies with which Sniffy performs his behaviors under five experimental conditions:

- A totally untrained Sniffy (a new Sniffy file).
- A magazine-trained Sniffy (the Sniffy file from Exercise 4 that we recommended you call Ex4-MagTrain).
- A Sniffy that has been shaped to bar-press (the file from Exercise 5 that we recommended you call Ex5-ShapeBP).
- A Sniffy whose bar pressing has been extinguished (the file from Exercise 7 that we recommended you call Ex7-Ext).

For each of these experimental conditions, perform the following actions:

- For the untrained Sniffy, start with a new Sniffy file. For the other conditions, open the file in question.
- Make sure that Sniffy is visible in his operant chamber. If necessary, select Show Sniffy from the Experiment menu.
- If the latest Cumulative Record is not visible, make it visible by selecting it from Cumulative Records section under the Windows menu.
- Select Behavior Repertoire from the Lab Assistant section of the Windows menu.

[5]The number of times Sniffy dismounts the bar may be less than the number of times he presses the bar if Sniffy presses the bar more than once before coming down off it.

- Click the Record button in the lower right-hand part of the Behavior Repertoire window.
- Select Isolate Sniffy (Accelerated Time) from the Experiment menu.
- Using the Cumulative Record as a timekeeper, record Sniffy's behavior for at least 30 minutes of program time.
- When 30 or more minutes of program time have elapsed, select Show Sniffy from the Experiment menu.
- Click the Stop button at the lower right-hand corner of the Behavior Repertoire window.
- Ascertain that the Behavior Repertoire window is selected by clicking on it once.
- Select Export Data from the File menu.
- Save your exported behavior repertoire data with an appropriate name on your hard drive.

After saving the four data export files, open your spreadsheet program and create a spreadsheet resembling that shown below.

			Relative Frequencies of Behaviors		
Behavior Category	Untrained	Mag Trained	Shaped BP	Extinguished	BP Training Effect
1) Rear - Front					
2) Rear - Back					
3) Rear - Side					
4) Groom Face					
5) Groom Genitals					
6) Tuck Head					
7) Turn					
8) Walk					
9) Sniff Hopper					
10) Eat Pellet					
11) Drink					
12) Sniff					
13) Fear Freeze					
14) Pain					
15) Press Bar					
16) Beg					
17) Roll					
18) Wipe Face					
19) Pause at Bar					
20) Dismount Bar					
21) Pause Raised					
22) Dismount Beg					
Sums					

- In this spreadsheet, the column labeled Behavior Category contains the list of Sniffy's behaviors. You can copy the list from one of your data-export files and paste it into Column A.
- Column F, which is labeled BP Training Effect, is where you will describe differences between the data in the column labeled Shaped BP and the data in the other columns.
- Open each of the data export files in turn and paste the data from the **Relative Frequency** column into the appropriate column on the spreadsheet that you have created.

When you have finished entering the data, the data in your spreadsheet should be similar to that shown next. However, because Sniffy's behavior is variable, the relative frequencies from your data files will not be exactly the same as those shown.

BP Training Effects.xlsx

	A	B	C	D	E	F
1	Behavior Category	Untrained	Mag Trained	BP Shaped	Extinguished	BP Training Effect
2	1) Rear - Front	0.020953	0.021726	0	0.021565	Decreased
3	2) Rear - Back	0.035171	0.035692	0.010241	0.032481	Decreased
4	3) Rear - Side	0.006485	0.004966	0.00033	0.005591	Decreased
5	4) Groom Face	0.082065	0.0928	0.012884	0.080671	Decreased
6	5) Groom Genitals	0.047393	0.049659	0.014205	0.042332	Decreased
7	6) Tuck Head	0	0	0	0	
8	7) Turn	0.494388	0.479516	0.344235	0.469382	Decreased
9	8) Walk	0.140434	0.145872	0.094813	0.148829	Decreased
10	9) Sniff Hopper	0.001497	0.000621	0.005616	0	Increased
11	10) Eat Pellet	0	0	0.185332	0	Increased
12	11) Drink	0.002744	0.004035	0.004295	0.003727	Increased?
13	12) Sniff	0.167623	0.164494	0.047902	0.193025	Decreased
14	13) Fear Freeze	0	0	0	0	
15	14) Pain	0	0	0	0	
16	15) Press Bar	0.000748	0.00031	0.185002	0.001864	Increased
17	16) Beg	0	0	0	0	
18	17) Roll	0	0	0	0	
19	18) Wipe Face	0	0	0	0	
20	19) Pause at Bar	0	0	0	0	
21	20) Dismount Bar	0.000499	0.00031	0.095144	0.000532	Increased
22	21) Pause Raised	0	0	0	0	
23	22) Dismount Beg	0	0	0	0	
24	Sums	1.000000	1.000001	0.999999	0.999999	
25						

Sheet1

Normal View   Ready

Basically, the data show what common sense would have predicted. As we would expect, when Sniffy has been trained to press the bar, the relative frequency of Press Bar is greater than in any of the other three conditions. The frequencies of Eat Pellet, Sniff Hopper, and Dismount Bar are also increased because these behaviors are closely associated with bar pressing. All the other behaviors, with the possible exception of Drink, are decreased. In summary, when Sniffy has been trained to press the bar and is being reinforced for doing so, the frequency with which he bar-presses and does other things associated with bar pressing are enhanced; and the frequency of everything else is reduced.

Something Else to Do

Another Effect of Magazine Training

If left entirely to his own devices in an operant chamber that has been programmed to deliver a food pellet each time the bar is pressed, Sniffy will train himself to press the bar. To find out how long it takes a completely naïve Sniffy to train himself to press the bar, open a new file, set up the program to deliver a food pellet for each bar-press, isolate Sniffy to accelerate time, and keep an eye on the Operant Associations mind window. When the Lab Assistant says that Sniffy is fully trained, mark the cumulative record (by choosing Mark Record from the Experiment menu). Repeat the process with the magazine-trained Sniffy that you produced in Exercise 22. Compare the times that the completely naïve Sniffy and the magazine-trained Sniffy require to complete their self-training. The magazine-trained Sniffy will self-train faster. Why?

6

Schedules of Reinforcement

Background and Examples

In extinction, reinforcement is completely cut off. This action simulates the situation in which a once available food source has ceased to exist. Another, even more common real-world scenario is one in which a response is sometimes reinforced and sometimes not reinforced. When a wild rat searches for food, there is no guarantee it will find food in the same place every time. The rat's searches are based on the probability of locating food. Going to a location where there once was food and finding none would not necessarily discourage the rat from trying there again at some other time when food might be available.

In a similar way, consider what your reaction might be if you turned on a light switch and the light failed to come on. How you would react would likely depend on your previous experience with that light switch. If the switch had worked reliably in the past, you would probably immediately go to look for a new light bulb. However, if the switch had sometimes required several flicks before the light came on, you would probably spend some time flicking it on and off before you decided that this time the problem was likely a burnt-out bulb.

With regard to Sniffy, so far we have discussed reinforcement as something that occurs either every time Sniffy presses the bar or not at all. However, you can also choose to reinforce only some of Sniffy's bar presses. The technical name for reinforcing every instance of a target behavior is **continuous reinforcement (CRF).** The technical term for reinforcing some, but not all, instances of a behavior is **partial reinforcement (PRF).** A rule that determines which instances of a response to reinforce is called a **schedule of reinforcement.** PRF schedules affect the temporal patterning of responses as viewed on a cumulative record. In addition, PRF schedules enhance resistance to extinction.

By enhanced resistance to extinction, we mean that if a response has been reinforced on a PRF schedule, the animal will make more responses during extinction than would be the case if the response had always been reinforced (continuous reinforcement).

The comparative effects of partial and continuous reinforcement on resistance to extinction can have real-life implications. Suppose that you are a parent of a young child. Many children who are about 2 years old develop a tendency to exhibit temper tantrums. In fact, this problem is so common that children in that age group are sometimes called the "terrible twos." How parents react to tantrums can have a profound influence on the duration of this phase of their child's development.

When a child has a tantrum, either you can reinforce the tantrum behavior by giving the child what he or she wants, or not reinforce the behavior by letting the child kick and scream until he or she gets tired and stops. (We assume you are not a person who would spank a child for tantrum behavior.) The best advice to parents of children who are just beginning to have tantrums is never to reinforce the behavior. If you never reinforce a tantrum, your child should pass through this phase quickly. However, many parents end up giving in to the child, especially if a tantrum occurs in public. The findings of operant conditioning suggest that if you are going to reinforce the behavior, it is better to do so consistently. That way, when the time comes to extinguish the behavior, the process should be faster than if you sometimes let the child scream and sometimes give the child what he or she wants.

Continuous reinforcement is the most efficient way to shape a new behavior quickly. But once the target behavior has been conditioned, continuous reinforcement is no longer necessary. Imagine the nursery school teacher's task with a new class of children. The children need to learn a great many new things—not only the prescribed lessons, but also social skills that will allow them to participate in the classroom. In the beginning, the teacher needs to reinforce the children's appropriate behaviors as often as possible. The teacher dispenses praise, stickers, and certificates and stamps stars on their hands. The nursery school teacher is a dispenser of reinforcers who at first must provide as close to a continuous-reinforcement schedule as is possible. However, this level of reinforcement is impossible to maintain, and children are soon exposed to a partial-reinforcement schedule. In first grade, children who know an answer to a question are expected to raise their hands and wait to be called on, and not every raised hand is recognized. As long as each child gets occasional recognition, the skills that they have learned will not disappear because, with partial reinforcement, it is difficult to extinguish their learned behaviors.

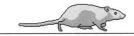

As noted, a schedule of reinforcement is a rule for determining which responses to reinforce. In their book *Schedules of Reinforcement*, C. B. Ferster and B. F. Skinner (1957) describe many different possible schedules. However, all these schedules are made up of combinations of two basic "families" of schedules: **ratio schedules** and **interval schedules.**

Ratio schedules reinforce the subject for making some particular number of responses. On a **fixed-ratio (FR) schedule,** the number of responses required is always the same. On an FR-5 schedule, the subject must make five responses for each reinforcement. This is rather like being paid for piecework, where the amount of money earned depends on the amount of work accomplished according to a prearranged pay scale. Because the amount of money earned is directly proportional to the amount of work performed, piecework tends to produce high rates of output.

When we observe animals on an FR schedule in the operant chamber, the pattern of performance seen on the cumulative record depends on the size of the ratio. Small FR schedules, which require only a small number of responses for each reinforcement, produce fast, steady responding. However, the performance of an animal that is being maintained on a large FR schedule is characterized by a pause after the receipt of each reinforcement, followed by an abrupt transition to rapid, steady responding until the next reinforcement occurs. As the size of a large FR schedule is increased, the pause after each reinforcement becomes longer. We can see something that resembles this pattern of responding in the behavior of a student who finds it difficult to start the next task after finishing a major assignment. The student's behavior is affected by the fact that a lot more work is required before the next reinforcement is obtained.

On a **variable-ratio (VR) schedule,** the value of the schedule specifies an average number of responses required to obtain reinforcement, but the exact number of responses varies from reinforcement to reinforcement. On a VR-5 schedule, the subject must make 5 responses on average for each reinforcement. Sometimes the subject must make 8 or 10 responses before reinforcement occurs, but these large values are balanced by occasions when reinforcement occurs after only 1 or 2 responses. VR schedules typically produce high rates of responding with no long pauses.

VR schedules are common in everyday life. Las Vegas–style slot machines pay off on a VR schedule, as does trying to arrange a date for Saturday night, or selling something on a commission basis. In all these situations, there is some chance or probability of success associated with every "response" that you make. The more often you respond, the more often you will be reinforced.

Interval schedules reinforce the subject for the first response made after a specified time interval has elapsed since the last reinforcement

was received. The time period during which reinforcement is unavailable begins when the subject receives a reinforcer. The interval thus specifies a minimum amount of time that must elapse between reinforced responses. On a **fixed-interval (FI) schedule,** the interval that must elapse before another response will be reinforced is always the same. On an FI–60 second schedule, exactly 60 seconds must always elapse after the receipt of one reinforcer before another response will be reinforced.

If your school is typical, every class period ends at a specified time. If you observe your fellow students, you will notice that their behavior changes as the time when the class is scheduled to end approaches. Early in the class period, everyone listens fairly attentively, and many students busily take notes. However, as the end of class approaches, students begin to put their notes away and prepare to leave.

On a **variable-interval (VI) schedule,** the time interval following reinforcement that must elapse before the next response is reinforced varies from reinforcement to reinforcement. On a VI–10 second schedule, the time interval would average 10 seconds. Few, if any, real-life situations are exactly equivalent to VI scheduling in the laboratory. However, trying to telephone someone whose line is frequently busy is similar to reinforcement on a VI schedule. Your call won't go through until the line is free, and the line is busy for varying periods. The difference is that on a pure VI schedule, once the time interval has elapsed, the reinforcer becomes available and remains available until the subject responds; but when you are trying to call an often busy telephone number, the line is busy and free intermittently. You can miss chances to complete the call by not trying often enough.

Each of these simple schedules produces a characteristic performance from subjects maintained on the schedule long enough for their behavior to stabilize. Depending on which schedule is involved, the animal may press the bar at a steady, predictable rate, or its response rate may vary in predictable ways. Prior to the appearance of the characteristic pattern of responding associated with the schedule, there is a period of acquisition during which the animal gradually adjusts to the schedule.

Variable-Ratio (VR) and Variable-Interval (VI) Schedules

Both variable-ratio (VR) and variable-interval (VI) schedules produce steady responding, but at different rates. VR schedules produce fast, steady responding. VI schedules produce slow, steady responding.

The difference between the performances maintained by VR and VI schedules is nicely illustrated in an experiment described by Reynolds (1975). The experiment involved two pigeons pecking at disks for food reinforcement in separate operant chambers. The experiment involved a **yoked experimental design,** which means that the behavior of the first pigeon could affect the other bird's reinforcement schedule. In the first chamber, pigeon A's disk pecking was reinforced on a VR schedule that the experimenter had programmed. In the other, completely isolated chamber, pigeon B's disk pecking was reinforced on a VI schedule in which the values of the intervals were determined by pigeon A's behavior. Each time pigeon A received a reinforcer for completing a ratio, a reinforcer became available for pigeon B's next response.

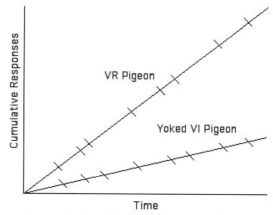

Idealized performances of two pigeons in yoked oparant chambers. Both birds peck steadily. However, although both birds receive the same number of reinforcements almost simultaneously, the VR bird makes many more responses.

The graph shows hypothetical cumulative records generated by two birds in this kind of experiment. Note that both birds respond at a nearly constant rate, but the bird on the VR schedule responds faster than the bird on the VI schedule. Although both birds' pecking behaviors are reinforced at virtually the same instant and although both always receive the same amount of reinforcement, there is a distinct difference in the rate at which they peck. This difference is caused by differences in the way in which the schedules interact with the birds' pecking behavior.

Fixed-Ratio (FR) Schedules

As shown in the next graph, the typical FR performance depends on the size of the ratio—that is, on the fixed number of responses required for each reinforcement. What constitutes a small ratio depends on the organism and the effort required in making the response. For Sniffy and other rats pressing a bar, a small ratio is anything requiring up to about 20 bar presses. For a pigeon pecking an illuminated disk, a small ratio is anything up to about 50. With small ratios, the performance is quite steady with no pause after each reinforcement. With large ratios, there is a pause after each reinforcement, followed by an abrupt transition to a high, stable rate until the next reinforcer is received.

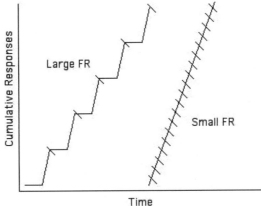

Idealized performances maintained by large and small FR schedules.

Fixed-Interval (FI) Schedules

Overall, FI schedules maintain rather slow rates of responding, more or less comparable to those maintained by VI schedules. However, whereas the VI performance is steady, the typical FI performance involves a pause after the receipt of each reinforcement, followed by a gradually accelerating response rate until the subject is responding moderately fast just before the next reinforcement is due. This typical FI response pattern, an idealized version of which is depicted in the next graph, is often called the **FI scallop.** As is the case with FR schedules, the pauses that occur after the receipt of a reinforcer are much more pronounced on large FI schedules than on small FI schedules.

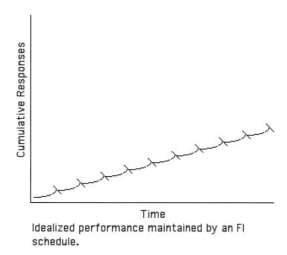

Time

Idealized performance maintained by an FI schedule.

Setting Up a Schedule in the Design Operant Conditioning Experiment Dialogue Box

Let's consider how to set up schedule experiments in Sniffy Pro. You establish different reinforcement schedules by choosing the Design Operant Conditioning Experiment command from the Experiment menu. When you execute this command, the following dialogue box shown appears.

When you are programming reinforcement schedules, you work with the left-hand part of the dialogue box under Reinforcement Schedule. Here is how the Reinforcement Schedule section of the dialogue box works:

- The Fixed and Variable alternatives at the far left determine whether the schedule requirements will be fixed or variable.

- The buttons labeled Responses and Seconds determine whether Sniffy is on a ratio or an interval schedule.
- Choosing Responses sets up a ratio schedule.
- Choosing Seconds sets up an interval schedule.
- You set the value of the schedule (the number of responses required or the number of seconds after a reinforcement before another response can be reinforced) by typing a number into the text box. As an alternative, you can also use the arrow keys to insert numbers into the text box. For example, if you wanted to set up a VI–20 second schedule, you would select the Variable and Seconds alternatives and place the numeral 20 in the text box.
- Selecting the button labeled Continuous sets up continuous reinforcement. All Sniffy's bar presses are reinforced. This setting is the default in effect when you first select a target behavior for the program to reinforce automatically.
- As you saw in previous exercises, selecting the button labeled Extinction sets up an extinction condition. If there is a check mark in the box labeled Mute Pellet Dispenser, the magazine sound is turned off during extinction. This is the usual way in which extinction is studied. If there is no check mark in the box labeled Mute Pellet Dispenser, Sniffy continues to hear the magazine sound whenever he presses the bar even though he no longer receives a food pellet. As we saw in Chapter 5, this nonstandard extinction setting enables you to study the secondary reinforcing power of the magazine sound.
- When you click the Apply button after setting up a reinforcement schedule, the Sniffy Lite program starts reinforcing Sniffy according to the schedule you have established.
- If you click Close, the dialogue box disappears and the program continues reinforcing Sniffy according to whatever settings were made before the Design Operant Conditioning Experiment dialogue box was opened.

Exercise 11: Placing Sniffy on a Small VR Schedule

Here are the steps that you should follow to place Sniffy on a small variable-ratio (VR) schedule of reinforcement. Except for the settings in the Design Operant Conditioning Experiment dialogue box, you would follow the same steps to place Sniffy on any small-value schedule.

- Before Sniffy can be placed on a schedule, he must first be fully trained to press the bar for continuous reinforcement. If you still have the file that you created after first training Sniffy to press the bar in Exercise 5 (the file that we suggested you name Ex5-ShapeBP), use the Open command in the File menu to open the file. If you do not have your original trained Sniffy file, you can use the file named ShapeBP located in the Sample Files folder.
- Look at the Operant Associations mind window. (If necessary, make the Operant Associations window visible by selecting it from the Mind Windows section of the Windows menu.) Make sure that the sound–food association, bar–sound association, and action strength are at their maximum levels. If you have opened your own file and discover that any of these measures is below its maximum level, you can let the program run until they reach their maximum levels before going on to the next step.
- Select the Save As command from the File menu to give the file an appropriate new name and save it where you save Sniffy files on your computer's hard drive. *This step is important because it preserves your original CRF-trained Sniffy for use in other experiments.* Because in this example we will be creating a file in which Sniffy is trained to respond on a VR-5 schedule, we suggest that you call the new file Ex11-VR5.
- Choose the Design Operant Conditioning Experiment command from the Experiment menu. Under Reinforcement Schedule, select the Variable and Responses alternatives. Type 5 in the text box.
- Click Apply.
- If you want to speed up the experiment, select the Isolate Sniffy (Accelerate Time) command from the Experiment menu.

Shortly after the Design Operant Conditioning Experiment dialogue box closes, your Cumulative Record window will look something like the following. Note that the Sniffy Pro program marks the point at which the VR-5 schedule was introduced.

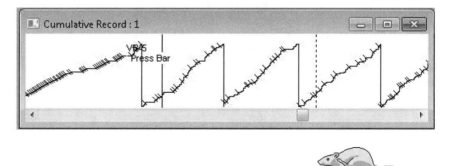

Immediately after being switched onto a schedule, when Sniffy encounters unreinforced responding for the first time, he will begin to extinguish. The Operant Associations mind window will display this process as a decrease in the strength of the bar–sound association and action strength. If Sniffy is fully trained on continuous reinforcement before you place him on a VR-5 schedule, he will not extinguish fully. However, if his continuous reinforcement training were incomplete, or if you tried to place him on a schedule with too large an initial value (such as VR-25), he would extinguish.

If Sniffy is going to adjust successfully to the schedule on which you have placed him, the bar–sound association and action strength will begin to increase again after Sniffy has received several reinforcements on the schedule. Sniffy is completely trained on the schedule when the bar–sound association and action strength approach their maximum values. At that point, Sniffy's cumulative record will be displaying the response pattern typical of the schedule on which Sniffy is being maintained. When you are satisfied that Sniffy's training is sufficient:

- Choose the Save command from the File menu to save your file.

Exercise 12: Increasing the Value of Sniffy's VR Schedule

Sniffy can be trained to respond on schedules with quite high values (such as VR-100 or FI–60 sec) provided these high values are approached gradually through intermediate stages. Here are the steps to increase the value of a schedule. As an illustration, we will assume that you are going to increase the value of the VR-5 schedule from the previous exercise.

- If the Sniffy Pro program is not running, start it.
- Use the Open command under the File menu to open your VR-5 file from Exercise 11.
- Check the Operant Associations mind window to be sure that the bar–sound association and action strength are at or near their maximum levels. If not, let the program run longer.
- Select the Save As command from the File menu and save the file under an appropriate name in the Sniffy Files folder on your computer's hard drive. Because we are going to be increasing the value of Sniffy's VR-5 schedule to VR-10, we suggest that you call the new file Ex12-VR10. Saving the new file under a different name preserves your original VR-5 file for future use if the need arises.

- Select the Design Operant Conditioning Experiment command from the Experiment menu.
- Be sure that the Variable and Responses alternatives are selected.
- Type the number 10 in the text box.
- Click Apply.
- If you want to speed up the experiment, select the Isolate Sniffy (Accelerate Time) command from the Experiment menu.

Because Sniffy is now experiencing longer runs of unreinforced trials, the bar–sound association and action strength will weaken at first. However, after Sniffy has received several reinforcements on the new schedule, these values will start going back up. When they approach their maxima again:

- Choose the Save command from the File menu to preserve your VR-10 trained Sniffy.

Repeat relevant parts of the instructions given above to shape Sniffy up to a VR-50 schedule. Sniffy will easily and quickly reach the VR-50 endpoint if you use as your intermediate steps VR-20 and VR-35. If you like to "live dangerously," try stepping Sniffy up to a VR-50 after VR-10 or VR-20. He may or may not extinguish with larger steps.

The cumulative record that you obtain once Sniffy has fully adapted to the VR-50 schedule should resemble that shown below. Note the rapid, reasonably steady response pattern.

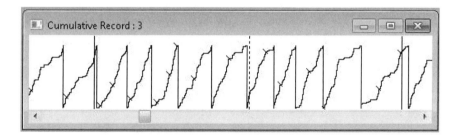

Exercise 13: Variable-Interval Schedules

Follow the generalized instructions given in the section entitled Setting Up a Schedule in the Design Operant Conditioning Experiment Dialogue Box to shape Sniffy up to a VI–50 second schedule. If you

want to speed up the experiment, select the Isolate Sniffy (Accelerate Time) command from the Experiment menu.

The cumulative record that you obtain once Sniffy has fully adapted to the VI–50 second schedule should resemble that shown next. Note the slow, reasonably steady response pattern.

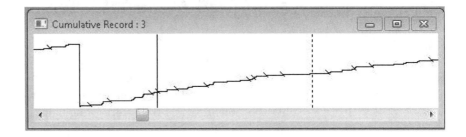

Exercise 14: Fixed-Ratio Schedules

Follow the generalized instructions given in the section entitled Setting Up a Schedule in the Design Operant Conditioning Experiment Dialogue Box to shape Sniffy up to an FR-50 schedule. If you want to speed up the experiment, select the Isolate Sniffy (Accelerate Time) command from the Experiment menu.

Note: With FR schedules, the Bar–Sound Association in the Operant Associations mind window will never reach higher than about 2/3 of its maximum value.

The cumulative record that you obtain once Sniffy has fully adapted to the FR-50 schedule should resemble that shown next. Note the pauses in responding that occur after each reinforcement is received and the abrupt transitions to rapid responding at the end of each pause.

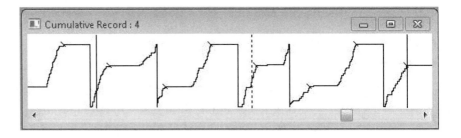

Exercise 15: Fixed-Interval Schedules

Follow the generalized instructions given in the section entitled Setting Up a Schedule in the Design Operant Conditioning Experiment Dialogue Box to shape Sniffy up to a FI–50 second schedule. If you want to speed up the experiment, select the Isolate Sniffy (Accelerate Time) command from the Experiment menu.

The cumulative record that you obtain once Sniffy has fully adapted to the FI–50 second schedule should resemble that shown next. Note the pauses after each reinforcement is received, followed by rather gradual transitions to moderate response rates shortly before the next reinforcement is due to occur.

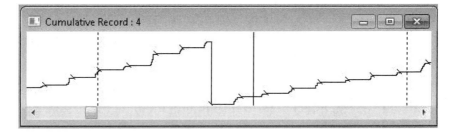

How Realistic Are Sniffy's Schedule Performances?

The speed with which Sniffy adapts to reinforcement schedules is one of the places where we sacrificed realism for convenience. Real rats adapt to schedules and changes in schedules quite slowly. In many instances, a real rat requires several daily one-hour training sessions before its pattern of responding in the cumulative record begins to resemble the response pattern that a particular schedule "typically" produces. Sniffy adapts to schedules and schedule changes much faster. We speeded up Sniffy's learning process so that you will have the opportunity to look at the effects of many different schedules in a reasonable amount of time.

Sniffy's schedule performances are not perfect replicas of the idealized performances shown in the first part of this chapter and in many textbooks on the psychology of learning. Idealized performances are designed to communicate ideas about what psychologists think schedule performances would look like if all the "noise" could be averaged out. The actual performances that you obtain with Sniffy and the actual performances of real rats are rarely ideal because the factors that tend

to produce ideal performances are not the only things determining the animal's behavior. For example, VR schedules are supposed to produce rapid, steady responding; and they tend to do so. However, pressing the bar is not the only thing that rats do while being reinforced on a VR schedule. Sometimes they take drinks of water. Sometimes they groom or scratch themselves. Sometimes they wander around the operant chamber for a little while. All these interruptions make actual VR performances less rapid and especially less steady than they would be if the only factors involved were those discussed in the first parts of this chapter.

Thus, the fact that Sniffy's cumulative records are not perfect replicas of ideal schedule performances means that, to a degree, Sniffy is behaving like a real rat. If you look at reproductions of the actual performances of real rats in scientific journal articles and in specialized books on reinforcement schedules, you will discover that Sniffy's schedule performances fall within the range of performances that real rats produce.

Exercise 16: The Effect of Partial Reinforcement on Extinction

Partial reinforcement dramatically increases a response's resistance to extinction. Animals whose responding has been maintained by a partial-reinforcement schedule make many more responses during extinction than do animals whose responding has been maintained on continuous reinforcement. In addition, ratio schedules tend to produce greater resistance to extinction than interval schedules; and variable schedules tend to produce greater resistance to extinction than fixed schedules. The Sniffy Lite program enables you to observe these differences in resistance to extinction. To measure Sniffy's resistance to extinction following partial reinforcement, you should follow these steps.

- Open a Sniffy Pro file in which Sniffy has been fully trained to respond on a moderate- or large-value schedule. We suggest you use a file in which you have trained Sniffy to respond on a schedule with a value of at least 25 (that is, VR-25, FR-25, VI–25 sec, or FI–25 sec).
- Look at the Operant Associations mind window to verify that bar–sound association is at or near its maximum level.

- Save the file under an appropriate new name (e.g., Ex36-VR25Ext) to preserve your original schedule file for future use.
- Choose the Design Operant Conditioning Experiment command from the Experiment menu.
- Click the Extinction option in the dialogue box; make sure there is a check mark in the box next to Mute Pellet Dispenser.
- Click the Apply button.
- If you want to speed up the experiment, select the Isolate Sniffy (Accelerated Time) command from the Experiment menu.
- Let the program run until Sniffy reaches the extinction criterion of no more than two responses during a 5-minute period.
- Save the file.

Print the cumulative record and determine how many responses Sniffy made and how much time elapsed before he reached the extinction criterion. Compare your partial-reinforcement extinction results with the extinction results that you obtained earlier when Sniffy's responding had been maintained by continuous reinforcement.

Exercise 17: Adjunctive Behavior

When Sniffy has been operantly conditioned to bar press or perform one of the other behaviors that he is capable of learning, the frequencies which he performs all the behaviors in his behavioral repertoire are affected. As you discovered in Exercise 10, the frequency with which he performs the behavior he is being trained to perform and the frequency of behaviors associated with eating increase. At the same time, the frequencies with which Sniffy performs most other behaviors decrease because he is busy performing the behavior for which he is being reinforced. However, psychologists have discovered that the frequencies with which rats perform behaviors for which they are *not* being reinforced also depend on the reinforcement schedule employed to reinforce the behavior that the rat is being trained to perform. Sometimes a behavior for which an animal is never reinforced may increase in frequency as a side effect of the schedule of reinforcement on which another behavior is being reinforced. Behaviors that increase in frequency as a side effect of the schedule being employed to maintain another behavior are called **adjunctive behaviors.**

Drinking is the adjunctive behavior that psychologists have studied the most. Rats that are being reinforced for bar pressing on interval schedules, especially fixed interval schedules, drink more often than they do when being reinforced for bar pressing for continuous reinforcement. Increased drinking as an adjunctive behavior is called **schedule-induced polydipsia.** To demonstrate drinking as an adjunctive behavior with Sniffy, we need to compare the relative frequency with which Sniffy drinks when he is being reinforced for bar pressing with continuous reinforcement and when he is performing on FI-50, VI-50, FR-50, and VR-50 schedules and continuous reinforcement.

- In this exercise, you will be using the Sniffy file from Exercise 5 (the file that we suggested you name Ex5-ShapeBP), the VR-50 file from Exercise 11, the VI-50 file from Exercise 12, the FR-50 file from Exercise 13, and the FI-50 file from Exercise 14.
- Open one of the files in question.
- Make sure that the current Cumulative Record is being displayed.
- Select the Behavior Repertoire submenu under Lab Assistant in the Windows menu.
- Click the Record button in the Behavior Repertoire window.
- Select Isolate Sniffy (Accelerated Time) in the Experiment menu to speed things up.
- After behaviors have been recorded for at least 30 minutes of program time, make Sniffy visible again by selecting the Show Sniffy command in the Experiment menu.
- Click the Stop button in the Behavior Repertoire window to stop recording behaviors.
- Make sure the Behavior Repertoire window is selected by clicking on it and then select the Export Data command from the File menu.
- Give your data file an appropriate name and save it in the place on your hard drive where you keep your Sniffy files.
- Compare the frequencies and relative frequencies with which Sniffy performs his behaviors under the five reinforcement schedules.

The easiest way to make the necessary behavior-frequency comparisons is to set up a spreadsheet resembling that shown below.

⬤ ⬤ ⬤	ScheduleRepertoire.xlsx	

New Open Save Print Import   Copy Paste Format   Undo Redo   AutoSum Sort A–Z Sort Z–A   Gallery Toolbox   Zoom   Help

Sheets   Charts   SmartArt Graphics   WordArt

	A	B	C	D	E	F	G
				Relative Frequencies of Sniffy's Behaviors			
1	Behaviors	CRF	VI-50	FI-50	VR-50	FR-50	
2	1) Rear - Front						
3	2) Rear - Back						
4	3) Rear - Side						
5	4) Groom Face						
6	5) Groom Genitals						
7	6) Tuck Head						
8	7) Turn						
9	8) Walk						
10	9) Sniff Hopper						
11	10) Eat Pellet						
12	11) Drink						
13	12) Sniff						
14	13) Fear Freeze						
15	14) Pain						
16	15) Press Bar						
17	16) Beg						
18	17) Roll						
19	18) Wipe Face						
20	19) Pause at Bar						
21	20) Dismount Bar						
22	21) Pause Raised						
23	22) Dismount Beg						
24	Frequency Sum						
25							
26							
27							

Sheet1

Page Layout View   Ready   Page 1/1   Sum=0   SCRL CAPS

After you have pasted the Relative Frequency columns from your five exported behavior repertoire files, the spreadsheet should resemble that shown next.

Relative Frequencies of Sniffy's Behaviors

Behaviors	CRF	VI-50	FI-50	VR-50	FR-50
1) Rear - Front	0	0.005642	0.000484	0.000213	0.000702
2) Rear - Back	0.010241	0.019882	0.015742	0.002554	0.010994
3) Rear - Side	0.00033	0.000537	0.000242	0.000213	0.000702
4) Groom Face	0.012884	0.068512	0.077258	0.004256	0.053099
5) Groom Genitals	0.014205	0.041376	0.062	0.003405	0.037895
6) Tuck Head	0	0	0	0	0
7) Turn	0.344235	0.454594	0.424558	0.108108	0.278596
8) Walk	0.094813	0.079258	0.062	0.037668	0.047719
9) Sniff Hopper	0.005616	0.096991	0.080649	0.019579	0.041404
10) Eat Pellet	0.185332	0.013702	0.0155	0.013407	0.007251
11) Drink	0.004295	0.033853	0.054977	0.002554	0.038596
12) Sniff	0.047902	0.088125	0.057157	0.012769	0.050994
13) Fear Freeze	0	0	0	0	0
14) Pain	0	0	0	0	0
15) Press Bar	0.185002	0.06475	0.111649	0.691211	0.367251
16) Beg	0	0	0	0	0
17) Roll	0	0	0	0	0
18) Wipe Face	0	0	0	0	0
19) Pause at Bar	0	0.004567	0.005328	0.014046	0.008655
20) Dismount Bar	0.095144	0.028211	0.032453	0.090019	0.05614
21) Pause Raised	0	0	0	0	0
22) Dismount Beg	0	0	0	0	0
Frequency Sum	0.999999	1.000000	0.999997	1.000002	0.999998

Because of the variability in Sniffy's behavior, the numbers in your spreadsheet will not be exactly the same as those shown, but they should be similar enough to show the same trends in the frequency differences for the different schedules and the various behaviors.

- The data show that the relative frequency of drinking is greatest when Sniffy is being reinforced on the FI-50 schedule, but the VI-50 and FR-50 schedules also produce more drinking than continuous reinforcement.
- When we compare the relative frequencies with which Sniffy performs other behaviors under continuous reinforcement and the other schedule, we see other adjunctive effects. These other adjunctive effects do not usually occur with real rats.

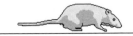

Questions and Things to Do

The exercises in this chapter barely scratch the surface of the things that it is possible to do with schedules of reinforcement.

Does Schedule Size Affect Overall Bar-Pressing Rate?

On an interval schedule, the schedule's "size" is the number of seconds after reinforcement before the next reinforcement becomes available. On a ratio schedule, the schedule's "size" is the number of responses required for a reinforcement. Exercises 32, 33, 34, and 35 ask you to set up, respectively, VR, VI, FR, and FI schedules of "size" 50.

Manipulating schedule size should have different effects for different schedule types. Pick a couple of different schedule types, such as VI and VR. Fully train Sniffy (so that the bar–sound association and action strength approach their maxima) to respond to values of 5, 10, 25, 50, and 100 for each of the two schedule types. Then determine the number of times he presses the bar during 30 minutes of program time and divide that number by 30 to obtain an average number of responses per minute.

- How does the response rate change as the value of the schedules increases?
- Does it change in the same way for the two kinds of schedules?

Does Schedule Size Affect Resistance to Extinction?

Pick a schedule type (VR, VI, FR, or FI) and fully train Sniffy (so that the bar–sound association is at or very close to its maximum value) to respond of values of 5, 10, 25, 50, and 100. Then determine how many responses Sniffy will make and how much time passes before bar pressing extinguishes with schedules of different values.

- How does the value of the schedule affect resistance to extinction?

7
Shaping Behaviors Other Than Bar Pressing

If you have ever watched circus animals performing, you will likely have seen the animals do a variety of "amazing" things that untrained animals of the same species do not do—things like bears riding bicycles or dogs walking tight ropes. Or you may have visited a roadside attraction such as the I.Q. Zoo in Hot Springs, Arkansas, where chickens jump through hoops and play baseball; and a duck plays the piano. One of the most important techniques that animal trainers employ to get animals to do these unusual things is shaping. To give you additional experience with shaping and to provide a bit of fun, we have enabled you to shape Sniffy to perform some interesting behaviors.

Shaping a live animal involves a number of steps. The first step is to establish a secondary reinforcer through a procedure resembling magazine training. The secondary reinforcer must be a stimulus whose timing you can precisely control. A common procedure used with dogs and many other kinds of animals is called "clicker training." You get a little noisemaker and teach the animal that whenever it hears the clicker sound, you will give it a small treat.

Before beginning to shape an animal, many trainers set up a **shaping hierarchy**—a sequence of behaviors that progressively resemble the target behavior more and more closely. At the bottom of the hierarchy is a behavior that (the trainer hopes) the animal will perform spontaneously and that resembles the target behavior in some way. When the animal performs this first behavior, the trainer starts out by reinforcing that behavior whenever it occurs. As a consequence, the animal will begin to perform the first-step behavior more frequently.

Animals do not always do things in exactly the same way. Their behavior is variable. Eventually, the animal will do something that resembles the target behavior more closely than was the case with the first item in the hierarchy. At that point, the trainer reinforces the

second-step behavior and requires the animal to repeat that behavior to obtain further reinforcements.

If the trainer is skillful and persistent enough, the process of reinforcing behaviors that resemble the target behavior more and more closely will eventually lead the animal to perform a target behavior that an untrained member of its species would never perform spontaneously and that looks spectacular enough to be impressive.

The exercises in this chapter will not make you into an expert animal trainer. However, they will provide you with practice taking Sniffy through short shaping hierarchies that culminate in behaviors that are fun to watch. The target behaviors that you can train Sniffy to perform are:

- Beg
- Roll (that is, turn a somersault)
- Face Wipe

To ensure that you succeed in shaping Sniffy to perform these behaviors if you try, we have provided lots of unrealistic help. The Sniffy Lite program will automatically record and reinforce target behaviors even though the behaviors do not involve interacting with a device in a way that would permit automatic recording with a live animal. And if you have trouble figuring out what to do, you can get help from the Shaping Tutor, which can be set to record and reinforce precursor behaviors for each of the target behaviors.

Disclaimer: The exercises in this chapter do not provide a realistic preview of what you can expect if you ever try to shape a live animal.

- To train Sniffy to roll or face-wipe, you begin by reinforcing grooming movements with a sound associated with food. Yet research with several kinds of mammals has shown that presenting food or secondary reinforcers associated with food is not an effective way of increasing the frequency of grooming movements (e.g., Shettleworth, 1975).
- Reinforcing a precursor behavior will cause Sniffy to start doing something else that is qualitatively different from (and we think more interesting than) the precursor behavior. In contrast, shaping a real animal ordinarily involves leading the animal through a large number of small quantitative changes that add up to a major change in behavior only after a protracted program of training.

Nevertheless, we believe that practicing with these simple examples will help you learn the *principles* of shaping. Just don't expect a real animal to be as "cooperative" as Sniffy.

Exercise 18: Shaping Sniffy to Beg

To see what the behavior that we call begging looks like, open the file named BegDemo in the Sample Files folder. Once you've seen what the target behavior looks like, follow the steps below to train Sniffy to beg.

- Open the file from Exercise 4 that we suggested you call Ex4-MagTrain.
- Select the Save As command from the File menu to give the file an appropriate new name (such as Ex18-ShapeBeg) and save it in the Sniffy Files folder on your computer's hard drive. *Saving the file with a new name before you start shaping Sniffy preserves your original magazine-training file for future use.* If your first attempt at shaping is unsuccessful, you can go back and try again without having to magazine-train Sniffy again.
- If Cumulative Record 1 is not visible, make it visible by selecting it from the Cumulative Record section of the Windows menu.
- Select the Design Operant Conditioning Experiment command from the Experiment menu.
- In the dialogue box that appears, select Beg from the Shaping Behavior section of the drop-down menu under Recorded Behavior. After making the selection, click on the Apply button to close the dialogue box.
- Note that the terms CRF and Beg appear in the Cumulative Record window. This notation means that the program will automatically reinforce every instance of begging and that the cumulative record will record begging movements.
- As your first approximation to begging, give Sniffy a pellet of food whenever he rears up facing forward (that is, facing you) anywhere in the operant chamber.
- After you have reinforced rearing up facing forward a number of times, you will begin to see instances of begging; and the program will automatically reinforce these.
- If you are patient, the time will come when Sniffy will beg 10 or more times during a 5-minute interval. At that point, you can stop shaping, sit back, and watch the progressive effect of reinforcement as Sniffy continues to beg more and more frequently.
- Sniffy is fully trained when the Action Strength column in the Operant Associations mind window approaches its maximum

with Beg as the automatically reinforced behavior. At that point, select the Save command from the File menu to preserve your trained Sniffy for future use.

After 45 to 60 minutes of attempting to shape Sniffy according to the instructions given above, Sniffy should be begging *at least* 10 times during each 5-minute interval delineated by the alternating solid and dotted vertical lines in the cumulative record. If your attempt at shaping fails to obtain that minimum result, something is wrong with what you're doing.

One possibility is that Sniffy has not been properly magazine trained. Look at the Operant Associations mind window. The sound–food association should be at its maximum level on the scale. If it isn't, either go back and repeat Exercise 4 to create a properly magazine-trained Sniffy or use the file named MagTrain from the Sample Files folder.

A second possibility is that you may not be reinforcing instances of rearing up toward the front wall as outlined above, or not reinforcing the behavior quickly enough.

For users who encounter difficulty with shaping, we have provided a section of the Recorded Behavior menu in the Design Operant Experiment dialogue box called the Shaping Tutor. If you are having trouble reinforcing Sniffy's rearing behaviors:

- Choose the Design Operant Conditioning Experiment command from the Experiment menu.
- Under the Shaping Tutor subsection of the Reinforcement Action menu, choose Rear – Front.
- The Sniffy Lite program will now automatically reinforce all instances of rearing up facing the front of the cage, including all begs. Watch which actions the program automatically reinforces.
- Once you've figured out what you were doing wrong, reopen the Design Operant Conditioning Experiment dialogue box and choose Beg from the Shaping Behavior section of the Reinforcement Action menu.
- Alternatively, if you are still unable to reinforce Sniffy effectively by hand, watch what is going on as the program reinforces front-facing rears automatically. Once Sniffy begs 10 or more times in a 5-minute period, reopen the Design Operant Conditioning Experiment dialogue box and choose Beg from the Shaping Behavior section of the Reinforcement Action menu. The program will complete Sniffy's training automatically.
- When Sniffy is fully trained, save the file.

Exercise 19: Shaping Sniffy to Wipe His Face

To see what face wiping looks like, open the file named WipeFaceDemo in the Sample Files folder of your Sniffy Lite CD. Face Wiping involves Sniffy touching his face with his paw and moving his paw up and down across his eye three times in rapid succession. The precursor behavior for Wipe Face is Groom Face, in which Sniffy touches his face with a paw but does not move his paw up and down across his eye repeatedly. Once you've seen what face wiping looks like, follow the following steps to shape the behavior.

- Open the file from Exercise 4 that we suggested you call Ex4-MagTrain.
- Select the Save As command from the File menu to give the file an appropriate new name (e.g., Ex19-ShapeFaceWipe) and save it in the Sniffy Files folder on your computer's hard drive. *Saving the file with a new name before you start shaping Sniffy preserves your original magazine-training file for future use.*
- If Cumulative Record 1 is not visible, make it visible by selecting it from the Cumulative Record section of the Windows menu.
- If the Operant Associations mind window is not visible, make it visible by selecting it from the Mind Windows section of the Windows menu.
- Select the Design Operant Conditioning Experiment command from the Experiment menu.
- In the dialogue box that appears, select Wipe Face from the Shaping Behavior section of the drop-down menu under Recorded Behavior. After making the selection, click on the OK button to close the dialogue box.
- Note that the terms CRF and Wipe Face appear in the cumulative record. These notations mean that the program will automatically reinforce every face wipe and that the cumulative record will record instances of face wiping.
- As your first approximation to face wiping, give Sniffy a pellet of food whenever he touches his face with one of his paws.
- When Sniffy has been reinforced often enough for touching his face, he will sometimes repeatedly wipe his paw across his eye instead of merely touching his face. This is the behavior we call Wipe Face, and the program will reinforce it automatically whenever it occurs.

- Each time Sniffy performs a face wipe, watch closely what he does after eating the food pellet. He may wipe his face again quickly after eating. If he does so, you know you're making progress. Allow him to continue face wiping as long as he will do so. However, if he does something else or touches his face without wiping, continue to reinforce face touching whenever it occurs.
- If you are patient, the time will come when Sniffy will perform a face wipe 8 to 10 times in rapid succession. At that point, you can stop shaping, sit back, and allow the program to automatically reinforce face wiping.
- Sniffy is fully trained when the Action Strength column in the Operant Associations mind window approaches its maximum. At that point, select the Save command from the File menu to preserve your trained Sniffy for future use.

After 30 minutes or so of attempting to shape Sniffy according to the instructions given above, Sniffy should be face wiping *at least* 10 times during each 5-minute interval delineated by the alternating solid and dotted vertical lines in the cumulative record. If your attempt at shaping fails to obtain that minimum result, something is wrong with what you are doing.

One possibility is that Sniffy has not been properly magazine trained. Look at the Operant Associations mind window. The sound–food association level should be close to its maximum. If it isn't, either go back and repeat Exercise 4 to created a properly magazine-trained Sniffy or use the file named MagTrain from the Sample Files folder.

A second possibility is that you may not be reinforcing instances of face touching as outlined above, or not reinforcing these behaviors quickly enough.

For users who encounter difficulty with shaping, we have provided a section of the Reinforcement Action menu in the Design Operant Conditioning Experiment dialogue box called the Shaping Tutor. If you are having trouble reinforcing Sniffy's face touching behavior:

- Choose the Design Operant Conditioning Experiment command from the Experiment menu.
- Under the Shaping Tutor subsection of the Recorded Behavior drop-down menu, choose Groom Face.
- The Sniffy Lite program will now automatically reinforce all instances of face grooming (touching), including all face wipes. Watch which actions the program automatically reinforces.

- When you believe that you are capable of effectively reinforcing these behaviors manually, reopen the Design Operant Conditioning Experiment dialogue box and choose Wipe Face from the Shaping Behavior section of the Recorded Behavior drop-down menu.
- If you still are unable to reinforce Sniffy effectively by hand, watch what is going on as the program reinforces face touching and wiping automatically. Once Sniffy face-wipes 8 to 10 times in a 1- or 2-minute period, reopen the Design Operant Conditioning Experiment dialogue box and choose Wipe Face from the Shaping Behavior section of the Recorded Behavior menu. The program will complete Sniffy's training automatically.
- When Sniffy is fully trained, save the file.

Exercise 20: Shaping Sniffy to Roll

The behavior that we call Roll involves Sniffy turning a somersault as he moves from left to right or right to left across the operant chamber. To see what the behavior looks like, open the file called RollDemo in the Sample Files folder.

Shaping Sniffy to roll involves a shaping hierarchy with two precursor behaviors: genital grooming and head tucking. You start out reinforcing instances of genital grooming. When the genital grooming has been reinforced often enough, head tucking will begin to occur. Head tucking is thus the second item in your shaping hierarchy. Once head tucking is occurring fairly often, you should stop reinforcing genital grooming and reinforce head tucking only. Eventually, reinforcing head tucking will begin to produce rolls. Finally, when rolls are occurring reasonably often, you stop reinforcing head tucking and reinforce rolls only. Eventually, Sniffy will have a high probability of rolling whenever he is in a position where he can do so without hitting a wall.

To shape rolling, follow these steps.

- Open the file from Exercise 4 that we suggested you call Ex4-MagTrain.
- Select the Save As command from the File menu to give the file an appropriate new name (such as Ex20-ShapeRoll) and save it in the Sniffy Files folder on your computer's hard drive. *Saving the file with a new name before you start shaping Sniffy preserves your original magazine-training file for future use.*

- If Cumulative Record 1 is not visible, make it visible by selecting it from the Cumulative Record section of the Windows menu.
- Select the Design Operant Conditioning Experiment command from the Experiment menu.
- In the dialogue box that appears, select Roll from the Shaping Behavior section of the drop-down menu under Recorded Behavior. After making the selection, click on the Apply button to close the dialogue box.
- Note that the terms CRF and Roll appear in the cumulative record. These notations mean that the program will automatically reinforce every roll and that the cumulative record will record rolls.
- As your first approximation to rolling, give Sniffy a pellet of food whenever he lowers his head down between his hind legs (as if he were grooming his genitals).
- When Sniffy has been reinforced often enough for lowering his head, he will sometimes begin to rock back and forth with his head tucked between his hind legs. This is the behavior we call Tuck Head.
- Reinforce all head tucks. At first, also continue to reinforce instances of genital grooming. However, when head tucking has become fairly common, stop reinforcing instances of genital grooming and reinforce head tucks only.
- When you have reinforced head tucking often enough, you will begin to see the first instances of rolling, and the program will reinforce rolls automatically. At first, continue to reinforce instances of head tucking manually. However, once you have seen a total of about 50 rolls, you can stop reinforcing head tucking. At that point, sit back and allow the program to reinforce rolling automatically.
- When the Action Strength column has approached its maximum value with Roll as the automatically reinforced behavior, Sniffy is fully trained. At that point, select the Save command from the File menu to preserve your trained Sniffy for future use.

You can expect that shaping Sniffy to roll, starting with a file in which Sniffy has only been magazine trained, should take anywhere from a half hour to an hour. So be patient and don't give up easily.

After an hour or so of attempting to shape Sniffy according to the instructions given above, Sniffy should be rolling *at least* 2 or 3 times during each 5-minute interval delineated by the alternating solid and dotted vertical lines in the cumulative record. If your attempt at

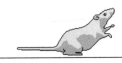

shaping fails to obtain that minimum result after an hour, something is wrong with what you are doing.

One possibility is that Sniffy has not been properly magazine trained. Look at the Operant Associations mind window. The sound–food association level should be at least three-quarters of the way up the scale. If it isn't, either go back and repeat Exercise 22 to created a properly magazine-trained Sniffy or use the file named MagTrain from the Sample Files folder.

A second possibility is that you may not be reinforcing instances of head lowering and head tucking as outlined above, or not reinforcing these behaviors quickly enough.

For users who encounter difficulty with shaping, we have provided a section of the Reinforced Behavior menu in the Design Operant Conditioning Experiment dialogue box called the Shaping Tutor. If you are having trouble reinforcing Sniffy's genital-grooming and head-tucking behaviors:

- Choose the Design Operant Conditioning Experiment command from the Experiment menu.
- Under the Shaping Tutor subsection of the Recorded Behavior menu, choose Groom Genitals.
- The Sniffy Lite program will now automatically reinforce all instances of genital grooming, including all head tucks and rolls. Watch which actions the program automatically reinforces.
- When you believe that you are capable of effectively reinforcing these behaviors manually, reopen the Design Operant Conditioning Experiment dialogue box and choose Roll from the Shaping Behavior section of the Recorded Behavior menu.
- If you are still unable to reinforce Sniffy effectively by hand, allow the program to train rolling automatically.
- When Sniffy is fully trained, save the file.

Exercise 21: Shaping Sniffy to Perform Other Behaviors

Manually reinforcing any behavior that Sniffy performs spontaneously will have the effect of making that behavior and other similar behaviors occur more frequently. Thus, if you are patient and have good timing, it is possible to train Sniffy to perform a variety of "tricks" other than those that we have documented in this chapter. One family of behaviors is something that we call sniffing. Sniffy sits with his head down near the metal bars that form the floor of the operant chamber

and twitches his whiskers. Four basic examples of this behavior form a family: sniff to front (Sniffy sniffs while facing you), sniff left and sniff right (Sniffy sniffs with his head pointed toward the left or right side of the chamber), and sniff rear (Sniffy's back is to you and he wiggles a bit, but his nose is invisible). Reinforcing any one of these behaviors will make the reinforced behavior and the other behaviors in the "sniffing family" occur more often. If you consistently reinforce any one of these behaviors and do not reinforce the others, the one that you reinforce will eventually occur much more often than the others. We invite you to explore and discover Sniffy's full repertoire of trainable "tricks."

Exercise 22: How Training to Beg, Face Wipe, and Roll Affects the Frequency of Behaviors in Sniffy's Behavior Repertoire

In this exercise, we will examine how training to bed, face wipe, and roll affects the relative frequencies of Sniffy's various behaviors. To evaluate the behavior changes, we will want to compare the frequencies after Sniffy has been trained to do his "tricks" with the behavior frequencies that Sniffy manifests prior to any training at all and after being shaped to bar press.

- In this exercise, you will be using the Sniffy files from Exercise 18 (the file that we recommended you name Ex18-ShapeBeg), Exercise 19 (the file that we suggested you call Ex19-ShapeFaceWipe), and Exercise 20 (the file that we recommended you call Ex20-ShapeRoll). In addition, to compare behavior frequencies after training to perform "tricks" with behavior frequencies after training to bar press, you will use the file from Exercise 5 (the file that we suggested you name Ex5-ShapeBP). To see how behavior frequencies following all these different kinds of training compare to behavior frequencies prior to any kind of training, you will also use a new, untrained Sniffy data file.
- Open one of the files in question (or start with a new data file).
- Make sure that the current Cumulative Record is being displayed.
- Select the Behavior Repertoire submenu under Research Assistant in the Windows menu.
- Click the Record button in the Behavior Repertoire window.

- Select Isolate Sniffy (Accelerated Time) in the Experiment menu to speed things up.
- After behaviors have been recorded for at least 30 minutes of program time, make Sniffy visible again by selecting the Show Sniffy command in the Experiment menu.
- Click the Stop button in the Behavior Repertoire window to stop recording behaviors.
- Make sure that the Behavior Repertoire window is selected by clicking on it and then select the Export Data command from the File menu.
- Give your data file an appropriate name and save it in the place on your hard drive where you keep your Sniffy files.
- Compare the frequencies and relative frequencies with which Sniffy performs his behaviors under the five reinforcement schedules.

The easiest way to make the necessary behavior-frequency comparisons is to set up a spreadsheet resembling that shown below, which depicts the relative frequencies of all Sniffy's behaviors under the five training conditions.

Relative Frequencies of Sniffy's Behaviors

Behavior	Untrained	Bar Press	Wipe Face	Beg	Roll
1) Rear - Front	0.020953	0	0	0.002323	0.00846
2) Rear - Back	0.035171	0.01082	0.011839	0.015099	0.019253
3) Rear - Side	0.006485	0.00027	0	0.00029	0.002334
4) Groom Face	0.082065	0.015418	0.080761	0.041812	0.094516
5) Groom Genitals	0.047393	0.010279	0.018605	0.030197	0.055718
6) Tuck Head	0	0	0	0	0
7) Turn	0.494388	0.349743	0.32093	0.459059	0.494749
8) Walk	0.140434	0.093048	0.054968	0.076074	0.080805
9) Sniff Hopper	0.001497	0.004598	0	0.00029	0.000875
10) Eat Pellet	0	0.190425	0.219027	0.088269	0.048425
11) Drink	0.002744	0.004328	0.013531	0.045587	0.0493
12) Sniff	0.167623	0.034623	0.059619	0.063298	0.096266
13) Fear Freeze	0	0	0	0	0
14) Pain	0	0	0	0	0
15) Press Bar	0.000748	0.190154	0.001268	0.001161	0.000875
16) Beg	0	0	0	0.088269	0
17) Roll	0	0	0	0	0.048425
18) Wipe Face	0	0	0.219027	0	0
19) Pause at Bar	0	0	0	0	0
20) Dismount Bar	0.000499	0.096294	0.000423	0	0
21) Pause Raised	0	0	0	0	0
22) Dismount Beg	0	0	0	0.088269	0

Because of the variability in Sniffy's behavior, the numbers that you obtain will not be identical to those shown, but your data should be similar. In the spreadsheet shown, data cells printed in boldface represent the training condition under which each behavior occurred with the highest relative frequency. Here are some interesting things to note:

- Five behaviors (Rear – Front, Rear – Back, Rear – Side, Walk, and Sniff) are most frequent in the Untrained condition, which represents the behavior of a naïve Sniffy prior to any training.
- Press Bar and Dismount Bar are most frequent when Sniffy is trained to bar press, findings that are exactly what we would expect. Sniff Hopper is also most frequent when Sniffy is trained to bar press.
- As we would expect, Wipe Face is also most common when that is what Sniffy has been trained to do. Eat pellet is also most frequent under this condition. A reason for this second finding may be that Sniffy can repeatedly wipe his face without needing to move away from the food hopper. (Note that eating is almost as frequent when Sniffy is trained to bar press, another behavior that he can repeat without moving away from the hopper.)
- The only two behaviors that are most common when Sniffy has been trained to beg are begging itself and Dismount Beg (a behavior that can occur only after a beg).
- When Sniffy has been trained to roll, rolling itself, groom face, groom genitals, turn, and drink occur more frequently than in any other training condition.

Exercise 23: Shaping a Cat to Beg or Walk on Its Hind Legs

Limitations in the Sniffy simulation mean there are limits to the variety of things Sniffy can be trained to do. However, animal trainers routinely use shaping to teach real animals to do an enormous variety of things that are physically possible but that an untrained animal would never do. As a simple example, training a physically fit cat to sit up and beg for food and to stand or walk on its hind legs without support is a fairly straightforward process even though untrained cats rarely, if ever, do these things.

Pet food manufacturers produce bite-size cat treats in several flavors, and it is often possible to find a flavor that your cat likes so much that the animal will work to obtain them. In fact, the cat may like them so much that you'll have to keep the treats container locked away to prevent theft. Once you've found your cat's favorite, the treats will constitute a primary

reinforcer that you can use to teach the animal to sit up and beg, to stand and walk on its hind legs, or to do other tricks.

As with Sniffy, the first step in training your cat will be magazine training. You need to find a stimulus that can be delivered with split-second timing when your cat does something right and that can be easily transformed into a secondary reinforcer by pairing it with treat presentation. Stores that sell party supplies often stock a variety of noisemakers, and many pet supply stores sell "clickers" that are designed to provide a sound that can be established as a secondary reinforcer.

You magazine-train a cat in much the same way that you magazine-trained Sniffy. To begin, wait until the cat is near you. Then operate the noisemaker and give the cat a treat. After you have sounded the clicker and given the cat a treat a couple of times with the cat very close by, walk a short distance away before sounding the clicker and giving the cat the next treat. You will know your cat is well magazine trained when you can call it from anywhere in the house (or neighborhood!) just by sounding the clicker.

Training a cat to sit up and beg or to stand and walk on its hind legs involves requiring the animal to raise its head progressively higher and higher off the ground before you reinforce it by sounding the noisemaker and giving it a treat. Start by watching the cat until it lifts its head somewhat higher than usual. (Standing with its front paws up on something doesn't count.) Then sound the clicker and give the cat a treat. After several reinforcements, the cat will begin walking around with its head held high more often. Because the cat's behavior is variable, sooner or later it will raise its head higher than your first criterion level, and that new higher level then becomes your second approximation that the cat must match to get additional treats. By the time you have reached the third or fourth approximation, the cat will probably be sitting on its hind legs with its front paws off the ground. Once the cat starts to lift its front paws off the ground, it will rather quickly reach a training plateau in which it sits up and "begs" for treats. Depending on your patience, you can either decide that sitting up is good enough or embark on the somewhat more challenging task of shaping the cat to stand on its hind legs and walk.

Once the cat is sitting up, it may or may not spontaneously start to stand on its hind legs. Some cats do, but many don't. If the cat just sits there without starting to rise up on its hind legs, try to elicit standing by holding a treat above the cat's head. Then, as soon as the cat starts to rise, sound the clicker and give it the treat. On the next trial, wait a bit before again eliciting a stand by holding out a treat. If you are patient enough, the animal will eventually start to stand on its hind

legs spontaneously. Finally, if you want the animal to walk on its hind legs, you will have to wait for or elicit behavioral variants in which the animal not only stands up on its hind legs but walks increasingly long distances before you sound the clicker and give it a treat.

If you decide to train your cat, you will discover that training a real animal is harder than training Sniffy. One reason for the difference is that your cat has a larger behavior repertoire than Sniffy; another is that the cat is free to move about and approach you in a way that Sniffy cannot. One difficulty will almost certainly arise: During magazine training, when you start to move away from the cat, it will follow you. If you sit down with the treats and clicker in hand, the cat will jump into your lap. If you are standing up and walking, the cat may jump on your shoulder. When these problems arise, don't punish the cat. You will significantly retard the learning process if you do anything to frighten the animal. However, if you never give the cat a treat unless you have first sounded the clicker, and if you never sound the clicker unless the cat is on the floor, the cat will eventually learn to stay off you and "cooperate."

"Clicker training" is also a technique that has become popular with many dog trainers. However, because dogs form stronger social bonds with people than cats do, enthusiastic verbal praise and physical affection are often the only reinforcers that dogs require. For a dog, the verbal praise probably comes to act as a secondary reinforcer that predicts the availability of physical affection. Whether treats should ever be used in addition to praise and physical affection is a somewhat controversial issue among dog trainers, but many dogs train faster when treats are used.

Another variant of operant conditioning that professional animal trainers use to teach animals to perform sequences of behaviors is called *backward chaining*. For example, suppose that you wanted to train a rat to climb a ladder, walk across an elevated plank to a door, and open the door to obtain food. You would first train the rat to go through the open door to the food, then you would shape it to open the door to get access to the food. The next step would be to place the rat on the elevated platform at the top of the ladder so that it has to "walk the plank" to get to the door. Finally, you would shape ladder climbing to get to the platform. In other words, the idea of backward chaining is first to train the animal to do the last thing in the sequence just before receiving the food. Then you make the opportunity to perform the last behavior in the sequence contingent on performing the next-to-last behavior, and so on. Most of the complex trained animal performances that you see in a circus or zoo are achieved through a combination of shaping and backward chaining.

Questions and Things to Do

- To get additional information about how the principles of operant conditioning can be applied in the real world, search the World Wide Web for pages dealing with "clicker training." You'll find numerous articles on how to train dogs, cats, horses, fish, and many other kinds of animals. Many people have a lot of fun training their animals to do an astonishing variety of interesting and useful things. You will also discover how operant conditioning is used to modify human behavior. For example, some coaches use clicker training to improve the performances of athletes.

- You can set up experiments on extinction, spontaneous recovery, secondary reinforcement, reinforcement scheduling, stimulus discrimination, and stimulus generalization using files in which Sniffy has been trained to beg, face-wipe, or roll. The results of these explorations will be variable. In some instances, you will obtain results that parallel those obtained with bar pressing. In other cases, you will get quite different results. Because the Sniffy program always uses the same neural network model of operant conditioning, you can be sure that the differences you observe are not due to differences in the underlying mechanisms of learning.[1] Instead, differences in things like scheduling effects and stimulus generalization must be the result of differences in the place the behaviors are performed and in the way the movements cause Sniffy to interact with his environment in the operant chamber. Think about differences between bar pressing and the other behaviors that might account for any differences you observe.

- Bar pressing is the only behavior in Sniffy's repertoire that involves interaction with a device (the bar). What is the importance of that?

- Bar pressing is the only behavior that must be performed in close proximity to the hopper into which the magazine drops food pellets. Is that important?

- Bar pressing can be repeated rapidly. For which other behaviors is that true? What factors limit the frequency with which other behaviors can be performed?

---

[1]We know that Sniffy always uses the same learning mechanism because we didn't give him any others. Psychologists often assume that animals always use the same learning mechanisms, but that assumption may not always be correct with live animals.

APPENDIX

How to Manage Your Sniffy Lite Files

USB Flash Drives

USB flash drives are small, portable devices that can hold substantial amounts of data. Here is a picture of a USB flash drive of the kind that can be used with contemporary Windows and Macintosh computers.

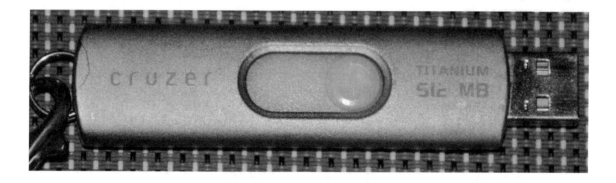

Many different models of USB flash drives are available with widely varying data-storage capacities. USB flash drives provide a convenient way of transporting data from one computer to another.

In addition, your computer contains at least one **hard disk** located inside the computer. The hard disks in contemporary computers usually have storage capacities of several hundred gigabytes (GB) (or more) of data.

Here are some tips that will save time and minimize frustration:

- **Always save your Sniffy files on the hard disk of the computer you're using.** The Sniffy Lite program is designed to save files onto and to retrieve files from the hard disk of the computer on which the Sniffy program is running. Saving files directly onto a USB flash drive or opening files stored on a flash drive often works fine but may sometimes produce unpredictable results.
- **If you don't have your own computer** and must store your Sniffy files on a USB flash drive:
  - Save your Sniffy files on the hard disk of the computer that you're using when you create the files.
  - Copy your files from the hard disk onto your USB flash drive when the experiment is completed.
  - Copy your files from your USB flash drive back onto the hard disk of the computer that you're using before you use the files again.

Where to Save Your Files

In Windows, the Sniffy Lite installer places the sample files in a folder called Sniffy Data Files, which is located in the My Documents folder associated with your user name on your computer's Local Disk (C).

The installation instructions for Macintosh told you:

1. To place the Sniffy Lite program in the Applications folder;
2. To create a folder called Sniffy Data Files inside your Documents folder;
3. To place the Sample Files inside the Sniffy Data Files folder.

We strongly recommend that you keep all your Sniffy data files together on your computer's hard drive. Keeping them together in the same place makes it much easier to find files when you need them.

Creating New Folders

To create a new folder in Windows:

- Point the cursor at the desktop or at an open folder window and click the right mouse button. (This operation insures that the new folder will be created in the right location.)

- In the drop-down menu that appears, drag down to New, then drag across to Folder, and release the mouse button. A new folder appears.
- Immediately type the name that you want to give the new folder.

To create a new folder on a Macintosh:

- Click your mouse button once while pointing at the desktop or an open folder window. (This operation insures that the new folder will be created in the right location.)
- Choose the New Folder command from the Finder's File menu. A new untitled folder appears.
- Immediately type the name you want to give the folder.

Getting Easy Access to Your Sniffy Data Files From Your Computer Desktop

Creating a Windows Shortcut

In Windows 7, the "ordinary" way of reaching the listing of your Sniffy files involves the following steps:

- Left-click on the Start icon at the bottom of your screen.
- Left-click on the word Documents in the right-hand panel of the Start menu.
- Left-click on the My Documents folder icon.
- Left-double-click on the Sniffy Data Files folder icon.

What a process! Fortunately, there is a simple way to reduce the number of steps involved: Create a shortcut to your Sniffy Data Files folder and place the shortcut on your Windows desktop. Here is what you need to do to set up the shortcut:

- Go through the four steps listed above to open your My Documents window.
- While pointing the cursor at the Sniffy Lite for Windows folder icon, click your right mouse button.
- A drop-down menu appears with a number of commands listed.
- Drag the cursor down to the Create Shortcut command, and click on it with your left mouse button.
- A folder icon with an arrow on it entitled Shortcut to Sniffy Data Files appears inside your Program Files folder.

- Click on the shortcut icon with your left mouse button, hold the mouse button down, and drag the icon onto your Windows desktop.
- Once the shortcut icon is on the desktop, you can drag it around and place it wherever you want it.
- In the future, all you have to do to open your Sniffy Data Files folder is to left-double-click the shortcut icon.

Creating a Macintosh Alias

For Mac OS X users, the easiest way of quickly getting to your Sniffy Data Files folder is to place an alias of the folder on the Mac OS X desktop. To place an alias of your Sniffy Data Files folder on your desktop:

- Locate your Sniffy Files folder inside your Documents folder.
- Click once on the folder icon to select it.
- Choose the Make Alias command from the Finder's File menu.
- A folder icon with an arrow on it entitled Sniffy Data Files alias appears.
- Drag the alias icon onto your desktop.

Saving Files

Let's imagine you have come to the point in the instructions for an exercise where we tell you to execute the Save As command and save the exercise with a specified name in an appropriate place on your computer's hard disk. Here is specific information about what Windows and Macintosh users need to do at that point in order to save the file in the Sniffy Data Files folder.

Saving Files in Windows 7

- Select the Save As command from the File menu in the Sniffy Lite program.
- A dialogue box resembling the one shown below will appear.

Save As   X

◀◀ Documents ▸ Sniffy Data Files   ▾ | ✦   *Search Sniffy Data Files*   🔍

Organize ▾   New folder   ▦ ▾   ❓

☆ Favorites
   ■ Desktop
   ⬇ Downloads
   ⬇ Dropbox
   ⊞ Recent Places

📚 Libraries
   📄 Documents
   ♪ Music
   ⊞ Pictures
   ⊞ Videos

⊛ Homegroup

💻 Computer
   💾 Local Disk (C:)

Documents library
Sniffy Data Files

Arrange by: Folder ▾

Name	Date modified	Type
SampeFaceWipe	08/06/2010 11:09 …	SDF File
SampleBeg	08/06/2010 11:09 …	SDF File
SampleMagTrain	08/06/2010 11:09 …	SDF File
SampleRoll	08/06/2010 11:09 …	SDF File
SampleShapeBP	08/06/2010 11:09 …	SDF File
SampleVR-25	08/06/2010 11:09 …	SDF File

File name: Untitled #1   ▾

Save as type: Sniffy Data Files (*.SDF)   ▾

▲ Hide Folders   Save   Cancel

- Look carefully at the dialogue box.
- At the top just below and to the right of the words "Save as" is a space containing an icon and the name of the place where the file will be saved unless you do something to change the location. In this case, the icon is a picture of an open folder, which tells you the current place is a folder. Different icons would appear for different kinds of places (for example, the desktop, a USB flash drive, or the root level of a hard disk[1]).
- In the large white space below the place name is an area displaying the contents of the place. Depending on what's in the currently

---

[1]The root level of a hard disk is the contents you see when you open a hard-disk icon by double-clicking on it.

displayed location, you may see names and icons representing files, folders, hard disks, or a USB flash drive.

- If the place displayed is where you want to save your file, all you have to do is to
  - □ Type the name that you want to give the file in the text box that is located to the right of "File name:".
  - □ Point the cursor at the command button labeled Save and click once with your left mouse button.
- If the place displayed is not where you want to save the file (for instance, if it's not your Sniffy Data Files folder), you can use the icons in the panel at the left-hand side of the dialogue box to find your Sniffy Data Files folder.
  - □ Remember that your Sniffy Data Files folder is the My Documents folder, which is also called the Documents Library.
  - □ In the Libraries section of the panel at the left of the dialogue box, click on Documents.
- Once you reach the Sniffy Data Files folder:
  - □ Point the cursor at the text box to the right of "File name:" and click the left mouse button once.
  - □ Type the name that you want to give the file.
- If you are using a version of Windows other than Windows 7, the dialogue boxes may look somewhat different; but the principles involved in saving a file in a particular place will be similar.

Saving Files in Mac OS X

We assume that you want to save a file in a folder called Sniffy Data Files that is located inside the Documents folder on your hard disk.

- Select the Save As command from the File menu in the Sniffy Lite program.
- Either an abbreviated or a detailed version of Save dialogue box may appear. The abbreviated version of the dialogue box is shown below.

- If the abbreviated dialogue appears, click on the button with a triangle in it that is located on the right end of the text box which appears after Save As:.
- Clicking on the triangle will cause the detailed version of the dialogue box, shown below, to appear.

Save

Save As: Untitled #1

Documents

Sniffy PB	Desktop ▶	eBooks ▶
SniffyPB	Documents ▶	Graphics ▶
	Library ▶	Microsoft User Data ▶
Desktop	Movies ▶	Miscellaneous*f* ▶
adhb	Music ▶	Sniffy Files ▶
Applications	Pictures ▶	Sounds ▶
Documents	Public ▶	Writs ▶
Movies	Sites ▶	
Music	Temporary Items ▶	
Pictures		

New Folder   Cancel   Save

- Look carefully at the detailed dialogue box.
- At the top to the right of the words Save As: is a text box into which you will type the name that you want to give the file. Because in this instance the file has not yet been named, the name Untitled #1 appears.
- Below the text box is a button showing a folder icon and the name of the location where the file will be saved unless you do something to change the location. In the example shown, the word Documents indicates that the file will be saved in your Documents folder unless you change the location.
- The main part of the dialogue box consists of two large white spaces separated by a vertical column. The area directly below the button

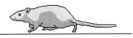

containing the name of the current location contains a list of places in your user area of the computer. Note that the word Documents and the icon to its left are highlighted. The highlighting is another indication that the Documents folder is your current location.

- The large white area to the right of the vertical bar displays the contents of the highlighted item in the left panel. In this instance, because the Documents folder is highlighted, the right panel displays the contents of the Documents folder.
- We assume that you want to save the file in your Sniffy Files folder. To do so, click once on the Sniffy Files folder in the right-hand panel. When you do so, the items that had been displayed in the right-hand panel move into the left-hand panel and the contents of the Sniffy Files folder are displayed in the right-hand panel.
- Once you're in the place where you want to save your file,
  - □ Type the name that you want to give the file in the text box under "Save As:".
  - □ Point the cursor at the Save command button and click your mouse button once.

Opening Files

Opening Files in Windows 7

There are several ways to open files in Windows, but we will describe only the most basic approaches. In the first example, we assume that you have already started the Sniffy Lite program and that you have just executed the Open command found under the File menu. When you execute the Open command, the Sniffy Lite program will always put up a dialogue box asking whether you want to save the file that is currently open. If you want to save the file, click on the Yes command button and go through the file-saving process. If you do not want to save the file (for example, because you've just started the Sniffy Lite program and there is no point in saving an Untitled file that contains no data), click the No command button. In either case, a dialogue box resembling the following will appear.

Open

« Documents ▸ Sniffy Data Files   ▾ | ↲   Search Sniffy Data Files   🔍

Organize ▾   New folder   ⊟ ▾   ⊡   ⓘ

Documents library   Arrange by: Folder ▾
Sniffy Data Files

Name ▲	Date modified	Type
SampeFaceWipe	08/06/2010 11:09 ...	SDF File
SampleBeg	08/06/2010 11:09 ...	SDF File
SampleMagTrain	08/06/2010 11:09 ...	SDF File
SampleRoll	08/06/2010 11:09 ...	SDF File
SampleShapeBP	08/06/2010 11:09 ...	SDF File
SampleVR-25	08/06/2010 11:09 ...	SDF File

☆ Favorites
　🗋 Dropbox
　🖥 Desktop
　⬇ Downloads
　🗐 Recent Places

📚 Libraries
　📄 Documents
　♪ Music
　🖼 Pictures
　🎞 Videos

🏠 Homegroup

💻 Computer
　💾 Local Disk (C:)
　💿 NO NAME (F:)

🖧 Network

File name: Untitled # 1   ▾   Sniffy Data Files (*.SDF)   ▾

                                                 Open ▾   Cancel

- In many ways, the Open dialogue box resembles the Save dialogue box. Here are the main things to note about it:
  - At the top of the dialogue box to the right and slightly below "Open" is the name of the place (the folder or disk) whose contents are currently being shown.
  - The icon just to the left of the place name tells you what kind of place it is. In the example, the open folder icon tells us that we are examining the contents of a folder.

- □ In the large area in the middle of the dialogue box is a listing of the contents of the place named at the top. You will see the names of the various items with icons that identify what kinds of items they are.
- □ When you see the name of the file that you want to open, point the cursor at its icon and click your left mouse button once. The name of the file will appear in the text box located to the right of "File name:" at the bottom of the dialogue box.
- □ When you've identified the right item, point the cursor at the Open command button and click your left mouse button once to open the file.
- A second way to open a file in Windows is to open your Sniffy Data Files and left-double-click on the file icon.
  - □ If the program is not running, it will start up automatically with the file you selected open.
  - □ If the program is running, you will be asked whether you want to save the file that was already open before the file on which you just left-double-clicked is opened.
- A third way to open a file is to drag the file icon onto the icon of the program or onto the icon of a shortcut to the program.
  - □ If the program is not running, it will start up automatically with the file you selected open.
  - □ If the program is running, you will be asked whether you want to save the file that was already open before the file on which you just left-double-clicked is opened.

Opening Files in Mac OS X

There are several ways to open files on a Macintosh, but we will describe only the most basic approaches. In the first example, we assume that you have already started the Sniffy Lite program and that you have just executed the Open command found under the File menu. When you execute the Open command, the Sniffy Lite program will always put up a dialogue box asking whether you want to save the file that is currently open. If you want to save the file, click on the Save command button and go through the file-saving process. If you do not want to save the file (for example, because you've just started the Sniffy Lite program and there is no point in saving an Untitled file that contains no data), click the Don't Save command button. In either case, a dialogue box resembling the following will appear.

In many ways, this Open dialogue box resembles the Save dialogue box. Here are the main things to note about it:

Open : Sniffy the Virtual Rat

Sniffy Data Files

DEVICES		
White Hall	Acrobat ▶	Sample Files ▶
SniffyPB	Adobe Reader ▶	
iDisk	AppleWorks User Data ▶	
SHARED	CBC Radio Freq ▶	
PLACES	ComputerStuff ▶	
Desktop	DrugInfo ▶	
antguy	DVDs	
Docume..	Hemo ▶	
Hemo	iPod & iP... Pix&Movs ▶	
Music	Manuals ▶	
Pictures	Microsoft User Data ▶	
RALUT	Office Projects ▶	
TCCF	RDC Connections ▶	
Sniffy	Sniffy Data Files ▶	
University	TCCF ▶	
	University ▶	

Enable: All Readable Documents

Cancel   Open

- At the top is a button containing the name of the place (the folder or disk) whose contents are currently being shown.
- The icon just to the left of the place name tells you what kind of place it is. In the example, the folder icon tells us that we are examining the contents of a folder.
- Clicking on the place name button will produce a drop-down menu showing the location of the current place in the hierarchy of folders and disks where there might be files that you could open and a list of folders in which you have recently opened or saved files. If you are not in your Sniffy Files folder, you may see it in the list of recent places. If it's there, you can select it from the list.
- In the large area below the place name button are two panels separated by a vertical bar. The panel on the left contains the place named at the top of the dialogue box. In the panel on the right is a list of the contents of that place. When you are inside the Sniffy Files folder, you will see a list of files and other items.
- Select the file that you want to open by clicking on it once.
- Then click on the Open command button at the bottom right of the dialogue box.
- A second way to open a file in Mac OS X is to open your Sniffy Data Files folder and double-click on a file icon.

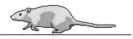

- □ If the program is not running, it will start up automatically with the file you selected open.
- □ If the program is running, you will be asked whether you want to save the file that was already open before the file on which you just left-double-clicked is opened.
- A third way to open a file is to drag the Sniffy file icon onto the icon of the program or onto the icon of an alias to the program. This is an especially handy way of opening a file if you have aliases of the program and your Sniffy Files folder in the dock. Just click on the folder icon to open the folder. Then drag the icon of the file that you want to open onto the program icon in the dock.
  - □ If the program is not running, it will start up automatically with the file you selected open.
  - □ If the program is running, you will be asked whether you want to save the file that was already open before the file on which you just left-double-clicked is opened.

Copying Files From a Hard Disk to a USB Flash Drive

Instructions for Windows 7 Users

- Open a window containing the file directory on the USB flash drive.
- If the USB flash drive is not inserted into your computer
  - □ Insert the USB flash drive into one of the USB ports on your computer.
  - □ In the dialogue box that appears, left-click on Open folder to view files.
- If the USB flash drive is already in your computer
  - □ Click on the Start button.
  - □ In the right-hand panel of the dialogue box that appears, click on Computer.
  - □ In the left-hand panel of the next dialogue box, double-click on the icon representing your USB flash drive (F).
- One way or the other, a window containing the file directory on the USB flash drive should now be open.
- Open a second window containing your Sniffy Lite Data file directory.
  - □ If you created a shortcut to your Sniffy Data Files folder on your desktop, double-click on the shortcut.
  - □ Otherwise:
    - □ Left-click on the Start icon at the bottom of your screen.
    - □ In the pop-up menu that appears, select Computer.

- □ In the Computer window, left-double-click on the hard drive icon.
- □ In the window that appears, select Documents from the left-hand panel.
- □ In the Documents library, left-double-click on Sniffy Data Files.
- □ Both the file directory of the USB flash drive and the contents of your Sniffy Data Files folder should now be visible in separate windows on your Windows desktop.
- □ In the Sniffy Data Files window, select the files that you want to copy onto the USB flash drive.
- □ Hold down your left mouse button and drag the file icon or icons in the Sniffy Data Files folder onto the USB flash drive directory window.
- □ Windows will copy the files onto the USB flash drive.

Instructions for Mac OS X Users

- Open a window containing the file directory on the USB flash drive.
- If the USB flash drive is not inserted into your computer
  - □ Insert the USB flash drive into one of the USB ports on your computer.
  - □ The USB flash drive's disk icon will appear on your Macintosh desktop.
  - □ Double-click on the disk icon to open the directory of the USB flash drive.
- If the USB flash drive is already in your computer, locate the disk icon on your desktop and double-click on it.
- One way or the other, a window containing the file directory on the USB flash drive should now be open.
- Open a second window containing your Sniffy Data Files file directory.
  - □ If you created an alias of your Sniffy Data Files folder on your desktop, double-click on the shortcut.
  - □ Otherwise:
    - □ With the cursor somewhere on the desk top, press the Command and N keys simultaneously.
    - □ Click the Documents icon on the left side of the window that appears.
    - □ Find and double-click on the Sniffy Data Files folder icon inside your Documents folder.

- Both the file directory of the USB flash drive and the contents of your Sniffy Data Files folder should now be visible in separate windows on your Mac OS X desktop.
- In the Sniffy Data Files window, select the files that you want to copy onto the USB flash drive.
- Hold down your mouse button and drag the file icon or icons in the Sniffy Data Files folder onto the USB flash drive directory window.
- Mac OS X will copy the files onto the USB flash drive.

Copying Files From a USB Flash Drive to a Hard Disk

This procedure is basically the mirror image of the procedure for copying files from your computer's hard drive onto a USB flash drive.

- Use the procedures described above to display both a window containing the directory of the USB flash drive and a window containing the contents of your Sniffy Data Files folder.
- In the window displaying the contents of the USB flash drive, select the files that you want to copy onto your hard drive.
- Drag the icons of the files that you want to copy onto the Sniffy Data Files window.
- Windows 7 or Mac OS X will copy the files from the USB flash drive onto your hard drive.

Using Sniffy Lite Macintosh Files on a Windows PC and *Vice Versa*

Sniffy Lite for Macintosh files are compatible with Sniffy Lite for Windows files and *vice versa*. You can create a file on one kind of computer and look at the file on the other kind of computer. You can even set up an experiment on one kind of computer, save the file when the experiment is in progress, and then complete the experiment onthe other kind of computer.

To transfer files from a Windows PC to a Macintosh

- Copy the Sniffy Lite for Windows files onto a USB flash drive.
- Insert the USB flash drive into a Macintosh.
- Copy the Sniffy Lite for Windows files onto your Macintosh hard drive.

- Start your Sniffy Lite for the Macintosh program.
- Use the Open command on the File menu to open the Sniffy Lite for Windows files.

To transfer files from a Macintosh to a Windows PC

- Save the files you want to transfer on the Macintosh hard disk with the ".sdf" suffix appended to each file name. To recognize them as Sniffy files, Sniffy Lite for Windows needs the suffix.
- Copy the Sniffy Lite for Macintosh files onto your USB flash drive.
- Copy the files from the USB flash drive onto your Windows hard disk.
- Start your Sniffy Lite for Windows program.
- Use the Open command under the File menu to open the Macintosh files.

Glossary

Acquisition In classical conditioning, the development of a conditioned response as the consequence of pairing the conditioned and unconditioned stimuli. In operant conditioning, the increase in the frequency of an emitted behavior as the result of reinforcing occurrences of the behavior.

Action Strength The part of Sniffy's operant conditioning algorithm, displayed in the Operant Associations mind window, that increases as a consequence of repeatedly reinforcing a particular movement.

Adjunctive Behavior A behavior pattern (responses) which is never reinforced but which increases in frequency as a side effect of the schedule on which another behavior pattern is reinforced.

Backward Chaining An operant training procedure used to teach an animal to perform an improbable series of behaviors. The animal is first trained to perform the last behavior in the chain that would occur just before reinforcement at the end of the series. Then the next-to-last behavior in the chain is trained by making the opportunity to perform the last behavior contingent on the performance of the next-to-last behavior, and so on.

Bar-Sound Association The part of Sniffy's operant conditioning algorithm, displayed in the Operant Associations mind window, that develops when manipulation of the bar is repeatedly followed by reinforcement.

Begging An operantly shapeable behavior in which Sniffy faces the observer, lifts up his front paws, moves his head up and down.

Behavioral Repertoire A list and description of all the behavior patterns that an animal emits.

Classical Conditioning The form of learning that occurs when two stimuli are repeatedly presented in a temporal series so that occurrences of the first stimulus predict occurrences of the second stimulus.

Clock Time Time as measured in the real world.

Conditioned Emotional Response A form of classical conditioning in which a conditioned stimulus acquires the capacity to elicit freezing and other fear-related behaviors as the result of being paired with an aversive unconditioned stimulus.

Conditioned Response (CR) In classical conditioning, the learned response to a conditioned stimulus which develops as the result of repeatedly presenting the conditioned stimulus shortly before presenting the unconditioned stimulus. In operant conditioning, an emitted behavior whose frequency has been increased as the result of repeatedly reinforcing the behavior.

Conditioned Stimulus (CS) In classical conditioning, a stimulus that has the capacity to acquire the capacity to elicit a conditioned response as the result of presenting the stimulus just before presentations of an unconditioned stimulus in a series of trials.

Conditioned Suppression An alternative name for the conditioned emotional response.

CS Response Strength The part of Sniffy's classical conditioning algorithm, displayed in the CS Response Strength mind window, that predicts the strength of Sniffy's response to the conditioned stimulus the next time it is presented.

Elicited Behavior   A particular behavior that occurs as the direct result of presenting a particular stimulus.

Emitted Behavior   A behavior pattern that an animal performs "spontaneously" and for which no eliciting stimulus exists.

Extinction   In classical conditioning, the diminution and eventual elimination of a previously conditioned response that occurs as the result of repeatedly presenting the conditioned stimulus without the unconditioned stimulus. In operant conditioning, the reduction in frequency of a previously conditioned response that occurs when the response is no longer reinforced.

Face Wiping   An operantly shapeable behavior in which Sniffy wipes one of his front paws repeatedly across an eye.

Fear   The part of Sniffy's classical conditioning algorithm, exhibited in the Sensitivity & Fear mind window, that predicts the likelihood that Sniffy will exhibit freezing and other "fear-related" behaviors.

Fixed Interval (FI) Schedule   A reinforcement schedule in which reinforcement of an operantly conditioned behavior is available only after a time period of a consistent duration has elapsed since the previous reinforcement.

Fixed Ratio (FR) Schedule   A reinforcement schedule in which an operantly conditioned behavior is reinforced only after a specified number of unreinforced responses, which is always the same for each reinforcement, have been performed.

Interval Schedule   In operant conditioning, a schedule of reinforcement in which a response can be reinforced only after a period of time has elapsed since the previous reinforcement.

Magazine Training   The procedure by which the sound of the food dispenser in an operant chamber is turned into a secondary reinforcer by pairing the sound with the delivery of food pellets.

Mind Window   A feature of the Sniffy program that displays certain parameters of Sniffy's algorithms for classical and operant conditioning. The parameters displayed correspond to psychological processes that psychologists have proposed as explanations for aspects of classical and operant conditioning. The mind windows show how changes in "Sniffy's psychological processes" are related to changes in Sniffy's behavior.

Movement Ratio   The proportion of time during the presentation of a conditioned stimulus that Sniffy is displaying freezing and other fear-related behaviors.

Negative Punisher   A stimulus whose removal as the consequence of a behavior makes that behavior *less* likely to occur under similar circumstances in the future.

Negative Reinforcer   A stimulus whose removal as the consequence of a behavior makes that behavior *more* likely to occur under similar circumstances in the future.

Operant Conditioning   A learned change in the likelihood that an emitted behavior will occur again under similar circumstances in the future that occurs as the result of the events that follow occurrences of the behavior.

Orienting Response (OR)   The initial, unlearned response to a conditioned stimulus.

Pain Sensitivity   The parameter of Sniffy's classical conditioning algorithm, displayed in the Sensitivity & Fear mind window, that predicts the duration of Sniffy's unconditioned response to the shock UCS the next time the shock occurs.

Pavlovian Conditioning   Another name for classical conditioning.

Positive Punisher   A stimulus whose presentation as a consequence of a behavior makes that behavior *less* likely to occur under similar circumstances in the future.

Positive Reinforcer   A stimulus whose presentation as a consequence of a behavior makes that behavior *more* likely to occur under similar circumstances in the future.

Primary Punisher   A stimulus whose capacity to function as a punisher is not dependent on previous experience.

Primary Reinforcer   A stimulus whose capacity to function as a reinforcer is not dependent on previous experience.

Program Time   Time as measured internally by the Sniffy program. When Sniffy is visible, the relationship between program time and clock time depends on animation speed. When Sniffy is hidden to "accelerate time," program time runs much faster than clock time.

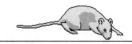

Punishment The operation of presenting a positive punisher or removing a negative punisher as a consequence of a behavior pattern, with the result that the punished behavior pattern becomes less likely to occur under similar circumstances in the future.

RAM Random access memory, one of the electronic components of a computer that in part determines whether or how well the computer can run a program.

Ratio Schedule A reinforcement schedule in which reinforcement for a response becomes available only after a number of unreinforced responses have been completed.

Reinforcement In operant conditioning, the operation of presenting a positive reinforcer or removing a negative reinforcer as the consequence of a behavior pattern, with the result that the reinforced behavior pattern becomes more likely to occur under similar circumstances in the future. In classical conditioning, the presentation of the unconditioned stimulus after an occurrence of the conditioned stimulus.

Reinforcement Schedule A rule that determines which instances of a response to reinforce.

Respondent Conditioning Another name for classical conditioning.

Response Measure Any measurement of the duration, frequency, magnitude, or probability of a behavior.

Salience A stimulus's ability to command an animal's attention.

Secondary Punisher A stimulus whose capacity to act as a punisher depends upon its prior association with a primary punisher.

Secondary Reinforcer A stimulus whose capacity to act as a reinforcer depends upon its prior association with a primary reinforcer.

Shaping An operant training procedure in which the animal is trained to perform an improbable target behavior as the consequence of reinforcing a series of behaviors that resemble the target more and more closely.

Sound-Food Association The part of Sniffy's operant conditioning algorithm, displayed in the Operant Associations mind window, that develops when the delivery of a food pellet follows his hearing the sound of the food dispenser mechanism.

Spontaneous Recovery The reappearance of a previously extinguished classically or operantly conditioned response which occurs when the animal is returned to the testing situation after spending time in another environment, such as its home cage.

Stage (of a classical conditioning experiment) A group of trials which must be completed before the next stage can begin.

Stimulus Generalization Responding in the presence of a stimulus that resembles, but is not identical to, the discriminative stimulus used in discrimination learning.

Suppression Ratio A response measure used to measure the conditioned emotional response. The suppression ratio is equal to the response rate during a CS presentation divided by the sum of the response rate during the CS plus the response rate during the period immediately preceding the CS.

Target Behavior The behavior that a trainer seeks to get an animal to perform at the end of shaping.

Unconditioned Response (UCR) In classical conditioning, the response elicited by an unconditioned stimulus.

Unconditioned Stimulus (UCS) In classical conditioning, a stimulus that has the intrinsic capacity to elicit an obvious and easy-to-measure response. In standard classical conditioning training trials, the UCS is presented after the CS.

Variable Interval (VI) Schedule A reinforcement schedule in which the period of time after reinforcement during which further responding is not reinforced varies from reinforcement to reinforcement.

Variable Ratio (VR) Schedule A reinforcement schedule in which the number of unreinforced responses required before another response is reinforced varies from reinforcement to reinforcement.

Yoked Experimental Design An experimental setup in which one animal's responding determines a second animal's schedule of reinforcement.

References

Annau, Z., & Kamin, L. J. (1961). The conditioned emotional response as a function of intensity of the US. *Journal of Comparative and Physiological Psychology, 54,* 428–432.

Domjan, M. (1998). *The principles of learning and behavior* (4th ed.). Pacific Grove, CA: Brooks/Cole Publishing.

Domjan, M. (2003). *Principles of learning and behavior* (5th ed.). Pacific Grove, CA: Wadsworth.

Estes, W. K., & Skinner, B. F. (1941). Some quantitative properties of anxiety. *Journal of Experimental Psychology, 29,* 390–400.

Falk, J. L. (1961). Production of polydipsia in normal rats by an intermittent food schedule. *Science, 133,* 195–196.

Falk, J. L. (1971). The nature and determinants of adjunctive behavior. *Physiology and Behavior, 6,* 577–588.

Ferster, C. B., & Skinner, B. F. (1957). *Schedules of reinforcement.* New York: Appleton-Century-Crofts.

Guthrie, E. R. (1960). *The psychology of learning.* Rev. ed. Gloucester, MA: Smith.

Hanson, H. M. (1959). Effects of discrimination training on stimulus generalization. *Journal of Experimental Psychology, 58,* 321–333.

Honig, W. K., Boneau, C. A., Burstein, K. R., & Pennypacker, H. S. (1963). Positive and negative generalization gradients obtained under equivalent training conditions. *Journal of Comparative and Physiological Psychology, 56,* 111–116.

Hull, C. L. (1943). *Principles of behavior.* New York: Appleton-Century-Crofts.

Hull, C. L. (1952). *A behavior system.* New Haven: Yale University Press.

Imada, H., Yamazaki, A., & Morishita, M. (1981). The effects of signal intensity upon conditioned suppression: Effects upon responding during signals and intersignal intervals. *Animal Learning and Behavior, 9,* 269–274.

James, W. (1890). *Principles of psychology.* New York: Holt.

Jenkins, H. M., & Harrison, R. G. (1960). Effects of discrimination training on auditory generalization. *Journal of Experimental Psychology, 59,* 246–253.

Jenkins, H. M., & Harrison, R. G. (1962). Generalization of inhibition following auditory discrimination learning. *Journal of the Experimental Analysis of Behavior, 5,* 435–441.

Kamin, L. J. (1968). Attention-like processes in classical conditioning. In M. R. Jones (Ed.), *Miami symposium on the prediction of behavior: Aversive stimulation.* Miami: University of Miami Press.

Keller, F. S., & Schoenfold, W. N. (1950). *Principles of psychology.* New York: Appleton-Century-Crofts.

Kimble, G. A. (1961). *Hilgard & Marquis' conditioning and learning* (2nd ed.). New York: Appleton-Century-Crofts.

Mazur, J. E. (1998). *Learning and behavior* (4th ed.). Upper Saddle River, NJ: Prentice Hall.

Pavlov, I. P. (1927). *Conditioned reflexes.* (trans., G. V. Anrep) London: Oxford University Press.

Polenchar, B. E., Romano, A. G., Steinmetz, J. E., & Patterson, M. M. (1984). Effects of US parameters

on classical conditioning of cat hindlimb flexion. *Animal Learning and Behavior, 12*, 69–72.

Rescorla, R. A. (1973). Second order conditioning: Implications for theories of learning. In E. J. McGuigan and D. B. Lumsden (Eds.), *Contemporary approaches to conditioning and learning.* New York: John Wiley.

Rescorla, R. A., & Wagner, A. R. (1972). A theory of Pavlovian conditioning: Variations in the effectiveness of reinforcement and nonreinforcement. In A. H. Black & W. F. Prokasy (Eds.), *Classical conditioning II: Current research and theory* (pp. 64–99). New York: Appleton-Century-Crofts.

Reynolds, G. S. (1975). *A primer of operant conditioning.* Glenview, IL: Scott, Foresman.

Rizley, R. C., & Rescorla, R. A. (1972). Associations in second-order conditioning and sensory preconditioning. *Journal of Comparative and Physiological Psychology, 81*, 1–11.

Schwartz, B., & Reisberg, D. (1991). *Learning and memory.* New York: W. W. Norton.

Seligman, M. E. P. (1968). Chronic fear produced by unpredictable electric shock. *Journal of Comparative and Physiological Psychology, 66*, 402–411.

Seligman, M. E. P., Maier, S. F., & Solomon, R. L. (1971). Unpredictable and uncontrollable aversive events. In F. R. Bruch (Ed.), *Aversive conditioning and learning.* New York: Academic Press, pp. 347–400.

Shettleworth, S. J. (1975). Reinforcement and the organization of behavior in the golden hamster: Hunger, environment, and food reinforcement. *Journal of Experimental Psychology: Animal Behavior Processes, 1*, 56–87.

Skinner, B. F. (1930). On the conditions of elicitation of certain eating reflexes. *Proceedings of the National Academy of Science* (Washington), *15*, 433–438.

Skinner, B. F. (1935). Two types of conditioned reflexes and a pseudo type. *Journal of General Psychology, 12*, 66–77.

Skinner, B. F. (1938). *The behavior of organisms.* New York: Appleton-Century-Crofts.

Skinner, B. F. (1953). *Science and human behavior.* New York: Macmillan.

Skinner, B. F. (1971). *Beyond freedom and dignity.* New York: Alfred A. Knopf.

Spence, K. W. (1937). The differential response in animals to stimuli varying within a single dimension. *Psychological Review, 44*, 430–444.

Tarpy, R. M. (1997). *Contemporary learning theory and research.* New York: McGraw-Hill.

Thorndike, E. L. (1898). Animal intelligence. An experimental study of associative processes in animals. *Psychological Monographs, 2*, No. 8.

Tolman, E. C. (1932). *Purposive behavior in animals and men.* New York: Appleton-Century-Crofts.

Index